THE EBONY ARK

OTHER BOOKS BY ERIC ROBINS

Animal Dunkirk
The Congo River
White Queen in Africa

ERIC ROBINS

THE EBONY ARK

Black Africa's Battle to Save
its Wild Life

TAPLINGER PUBLISHING COMPANY
NEW YORK

First Published in the United States in 1970 by
TAPLINGER PUBLISHING CO., INC.
New York, New York

Copyright © 1970 BY ERIC ROBINS

ISBN 0-8008-2360-5

Library of Congress Catalog Number 70-125 931

PRINTED IN GREAT BRITAIN

CONTENTS

List of Illustrations

Author's Note

Foreword
by His Excellency Dr Kenneth D. Kaunda,
President of the Republic of Zambia

Introduction

"This Precious Inheritance"   1
Under the Black Star   11
Abuko   19
Hugo the Hippo   29
Tears for Crocodiles   38
Elephant in Casserole   49
Underwater Zoos   60
"Let Us Not Regret"   69
SOS—Grasshoppers!   78
Exit Obongi   90
Rhinos on Wheels   98
Leopards' Tragedy   108
Goodbye Masai   122
The Man who talks to Lions   132
A Quintet of Custodians   143
"Animal Interpol"   154
The Way Ahead   162
Epilogue   171
Index   181

v

ILLUSTRATIONS

	Facing page
Dr Kenneth Kaunda, President of Zambia	12
Ranger force heading for the bush in Tanzania	13
Zebra in Serengeti	13
Snares and hacked-up victims found in a poachers' camp	28
A poacher's grass hut set ablaze	28

Between pages 28 & 29
Loading poached ivory aboard a dug-out canoe
Giraffe and zebra form bizarre patterns

Field force arresting poachers in Tsavo	29
Woebegone poacher, under arrest	29
Field force take prisoners back to headquarters	29
A captured rhino poacher	44
Samuel Ayodo, Kenya's former Minister of Tourism and Wildlife	44

Between pages 44 & 45
A young civet cat in Abuko Nature Reserve
Orphanage ranger with baby cheetah

Francis X. Katete, Director of National Parks, Uganda	45
Anti-poaching patrol on Uganda's Victoria Nile	45
Dr Julius Nyerere and Emperor Haile Selassie at Lake Manyara, Tanzania	60
Solomon ole Saibull, Conservator of Ngorongoro Crater	60

Between pages 60 & 61
Kenya's President Jomo Kenyatta watching elephant
African delegates to wild life conference at Kilaguni Lodge
A gorilla in the Congo (Kinshasa)

Nairobi National Park rangers	61
Baby cheetah	61
A young monkey in the Animal Orphanage, Nairobi	76
Buffalo in the Orphanage	76

Between pages 76 & 77
The crocodile pool in Abuko
Sylvester Ruhweza, Chief Game Warden, Uganda
Buffalo staring at the camera

Facing Page

Two young cheetah in the Nairobi National Park   77
A leopard with its prey   92

Between pages 92 & 93
Nairobi's Orphanage sign
Mr Samuel Ngethe feeds a wildebeeste calf
Hostel at Seronera in Tanzania's Serengeti National Park
Tanzania's intensive wild life education campaign

A line-up of giraffe   93
Kenyan Cabinet Minister, Dr Julius Kiano, at Treetops   93
One of the tree-roosting lions of East Africa   108

Between pages 108 & 109
Rhino at Treetops
President Kenyatta and Emperor Haile Selassie at Tree-
    tops
A leopard fixes a cold green eye on observers

Perez Olindo, Director of National Parks, Kenya, in a
    light plane   109
A £52,000 haul of poached ivory, rhino horns, leopard
    skins and other trophies   109
The Wildlife Education bus in Nairobi National Park   124
A rhino watched by African schoolchildren   124

Between pages 124 & 125
Christopher Manu of Ghana
An old bull elephant at the foot of Mount Kilimanjaro
A hungry leopard
Students at the College of African Wildlife Manage-
    ment, Mweka, Tanzania

Masai warrior   125

Emperor Haile Selassie feeds a young gazelle   140
Zebra gallop along a dirt road in Serengeti   140
A young West African green vervet monkey   141

AUTHOR'S NOTE

In addition to the field personalities featured in the chapters ahead, my warmest thanks for their valuable co-operation in the preparation of this book are extended to Miss Marion Kaplan; Gemini News Service; the African Wildlife Leadership Foundation; Mr. Philip Short; Mr. Hugh Russell; Loomis Dean of *Life* magazine; Mr. Don Diment; Miss Valerie Robins; Mr. Henry Reuter, Editor of *Safari* magazine; the Principal and Staff of the College of African Wildlife Management, Mweka, Tanzania; Mr. Peter Darling, Editor of the *Sunday Nation*, Nairobi (for permission to use extracts from an interview with the Director of National Parks in Uganda), Mr. Norman Myers, Mr. Martin Meredith, Mr. John Pile of the United Nations, Dr Andreas von Nagy, and Mr. Dunstan Kamana.

"What human being is able to create new animals? Once they are gone, they are gone forever." *Extract from an African schoolboy's essay on game conservation.*

"The more the rest of the world poisons itself with pollution, buries all pleasures of life under concrete and substitutes engine, wheel and brake screams for the charm of mammal, bird and frog calls, the more African countries which protect their wild animals will stand out as monuments of Man's resistance to Man's destructiveness." *A Canadian zoologist.*

FOREWORD

BY HIS EXCELLENCY DR. KENNETH D. KAUNDA,

PRESIDENT OF THE REPUBLIC OF ZAMBIA

I am very happy indeed to be asked to write a foreword for a book which reviews and records with such evident appreciation the efforts of most independent African States to protect and preserve for future generations their rich but dwindling heritage of wild life.

Africa still has regrettably few defenders outside the boundaries of this continent and it is, therefore, even more encouraging to me to read a book of this kind and to have an opportunity to help to establish it on the bookshelves of the world.

In the final analysis, of course, it is the Governments and peoples of Africa upon whom the responsibility and burden of conserving the natural resources of their continent must lie; and, in this book, with its descriptions of the battles against poachers, the struggles to preserve dying species and the efforts to re-educate rural peoples, the author has been able to show clearly how, in accordance with the O.A.U. Algiers Convention of 1968, my colleagues and comrades in free Governments throughout our beloved continent, are responding earnestly, enthusiastically and with selfless dedication to this challenge.

I should, however, take this opportunity to add this word of caution. Although the author quite rightly, and indeed very vividly, points out the most commendable work that a number of free Governments are carrying out in this rather important field, we are very conscious of a number of shortcomings :

Firstly,   Most of the experiments that we are carrying out are new not only to us but to the rest of mankind and we are, therefore, very anxious that, in our eagerness to discharge our responsibilities, we will not unwittingly cause more destruction to the wild life we are so anxious to utilise in a responsible manner.

Secondly,   We have very limited resources, both human as well as material, to enable us to meet what is obviously an overwhelming problem. Nevertheless, with the many experienced people and organisations, some of whom the author has mentioned, showing willingness to come to our aid, I believe that we stand a good chance of succeeding.

Finally, I sincerely hope that this work will serve as a source of inspiration to African leaders and their people as well as a clear demonstration to many outside Africa of the serious view we take of our responsibilities, not only to our own people, but to mankind as a whole. The continuous preservation of wild life must be the constant preoccupation of Man.

KENNETH D. KAUNDA

State House,
Lusaka.
30th November, 1969.

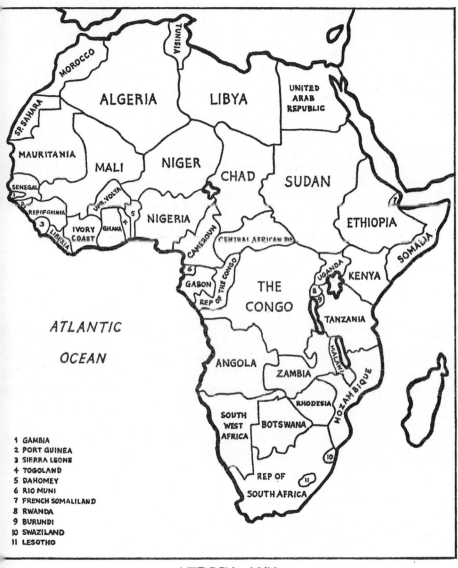

1 GAMBIA
2 PORT GUINEA
3 SIERRA LEONE
4 TOGOLAND
5 DAHOMEY
6 RIO MUNI
7 FRENCH SOMALILAND
8 RWANDA
9 BURUNDI
10 SWAZILAND
11 LESOTHO

AFRICA 1970

INTRODUCTION

Black hands are today the guardians of what remains of Africa's majestic and enchanting wild life.

Several years ago, I wrote (for *Life* magazine after a tour of several African countries about to become independent): "Africa's game, mankind's wealth of variety and beauty represented by a dwindling throng of the most varied and fantastic kinds of animals found anywhere on earth, faces a total eclipse. Preservation of the wild animals, part of the balance of Nature on which our existence depends, is a challenge to Man's self-respect."

It is now generally accepted, by all except the rabidly prejudiced, that most of the governments of Africans have tipped the post-freedom scales in favour of an upswing of general game conservation, aided by British, American and international funds.

"Gloomy forecasts that the country's wild life was heading for extinction once Africans took over have been proved wrong," Kenya's Minister for Tourism and Wildlife said proudly. "The game in some areas is now more plentiful than in the pre-independence days, and the Kenya Government itself has made great progress in the development of existing national parks and the formation of new ones.

"Apart from national considerations, we feel we have a duty to mankind to ensure the survival of wild life for the people of all races of the world for all time."

That the raw and spectacularly primeval still exists in significant degree in many newly-independent countries is due in large measure to the foresight of the black leaders. Accordingly, the nations which but a few years ago stood on the threshold of their freedoms have shown themselves acutely aware—whether principally from self-interest or not—of the key factors to be implemented in nuturing the surviving 10% or so of Africa's once staggering game numbers.

In spite of the fears of many Western wiseacres at the end of the colonial periods that there would be wholesale neglect, what remains of each African country's legacy of game animals is being both conscientiously conserved and fostered from the dividends of tourism wild life generates.

The sanctuaries first established by the white man continue to be efficiently maintained, extended when and where necessary, and, by and large, outstandingly well managed—even while the authorities are often obliged to alleviate the land hunger of the tribespeople in keeping with continuing population explosions. In general, only if the overriding interests of the game will not run counter to human interests can an area be designated as a national park or a similar protected section of a country. But in such reserves the preservation of fauna takes precedence over all other interests.

Somewhere in Africa, new game havens are being created almost every year.

The fledgling regimes are ensuring vital water conservation—with the building of dams and courses—to keep the animals alive in seasonal droughts. Antierosion measures against subsequent floods are constantly being extended in the game strongholds. Some efficiently organised conservation campaigns have made appreciable inroads on the traditional outlook of hosts of grass-roots tribesmen that wild animals were but "leaping meat" on the hoof to be slaughtered freely on sight.

African adults with even only a basic education have long since got over their attitude of regarding game parks and controlled areas as mere relics of colonialism.

In maintaining the animal sanctuaries, and enlarging them where possible, governments recognise their propagandistic as well as monetary worth. Model game parks serve to give the lie to racial slanders that Africans continue to be "cruel and uncivilised."

Rapidly increasing numbers of tourists from all over the globe are being attracted in super-airliners to Africa's *safari* lands, providing more funds for increased staffs and equipment in the various national parks and animal reserves.

Nomadic tribespeople are being taught by their more enlightened fellow Africans to settle down increasingly in agricultural communities and to give up the deadly over-grazing of their large herds of cattle on the game plains.

Elephant and hippo continue to be humanely and scientifically culled in areas in African countries where swollen populations of these animals have gravely thinned the habitat of their own herds, and possibly that of other species.

Thousands of devoted Africans have become game rangers ("They have something of the martyrs in their make-up, scorning personal riches and living in conditions of hardship and virtual penance to be among their charges," as one white hunter puts it). As such they have become the courageous and relentless enemies of their murderous "brothers" who are poachers.

"The game animals of Africa have stirred the imagination of men in other lands with their promise of adventure," said a charcoal-skinned game warden, one of Africa's own new breed of conservationists. "Nowhere else can one still see such an abundance and variety of animals in their natural setting. We have good climates, beautiful scenery, snow-capped mountains, the attractions of the coasts, and many picturesque scenes of African life. It is these we can set against the cathedrals and art galleries as our contribution to the cultural heritage of mankind."
Nairobi: February, 1970.

"This Precious Inheritance"

The trembling 19-year-old African from Ghana stood, unarmed, behind a slender thorn tree and sketched a family of rhino less than 50 feet away. His companion slipped back the safety-catch of a high-powered sporting gun and prepared to face a charging rogue elephant.

Another youngster (from a tribal settlement in northern Uganda) solemnly recited the hazardous drill of tracking down game poachers armed with rifles and spears. A perspiring, brawny Zambian who emerged from the tall grass had for an hour been going through the motions of stalking a man-eating lion.

These scenes and situations reflect a routine day in the field for the pupils of the only school of its kind in the world—the handsomely brick-built College of African Wildlife Management, over which looms Mount Kilimanjaro in all its majesty, at Mweka in Tanzania.

Founded in 1963, the College, whose sponsoring

agency is the Organisation for African Unity and which draws financial aid from such international sources as the United Nations Special Fund, the Ford Foundation, the British Ministry of Overseas Development, and the African Wildlife Leadership Foundation, has become one of Africa's most vigorous and significant institutions.

It is the *alma mater* of many Africans now leaders in the various fields of wild animal husbandry across the Continent.

"The animals and the lands which they inhabit are a major natural resource," states Mweka's charter, "and, properly managed and conserved, they can be of great economic, aesthetic and educational value to the African countries. The future of this resource, therefore, must rest in the hands of the people who are trained in wild life management on a scientific basis if conservation of the animals and their habitat is to be achieved."

This echoes a ringing declaration—believed to have been the first then of its kind in history—which was made by the leader of Tanganyika (now Tanzania), Julius Nyerere, a long-standing champion of African wild life, on the eve of his country's independence at the end of 1961. At an international conference of game experts, ecologists and other scientists in torrid and teeming little Arusha, some 40 miles from Mweka, Nyerere formally accepted trusteeship of the nation's wild herds and the responsibility for their preservation.

His manifesto read: "We solemnly declare that we will do everything in our power to make sure that our children's grandchildren will be able to enjoy this rich and precious inheritance. The survival of our wild life is a matter of grave concern to all of us in Africa. These wild creatures are not only important as a source of wonder and inspiration, but are an integral part of our natural resources and of our future livelihood and well-being."

The Arusha conference agreed that, as impending grants of independence would be followed by accelerated Africanisation, a centre was urgently needed to provide suitably trained persons for higher-grade Game and National Parks departments' posts.

To this end the College of African Wildlife Management was established. It was soon to become a landmark in the chronicles of game conservation in emergent Africa.

At the end of the first year of a two-year course for senior posts, eighteen students were in training— eight from Tanganyika, four from Kenya Game Department, three from the Uganda Game Division and one from Uganda National Parks, one from Nyasaland (now Malawi) Forestry Department, and another from the West Cameroon Forest Department.

A second course lasting nine months and held once a year was introduced later to turn out African middle-grade game officials, and at the start of the second of these courses thirty students from Tanzania alone were enrolled.

At the June, 1968, graduation ceremony at the College, forty-six students were presented with diplomas and certificates after successfully completing their courses. Eleven students took the two-year diploma course, and thirty-five completed the one-year certificate course. An Ethiopian won the award for the best all-round performance.

By that time, 145 students from all over black

Africa had qualified at the College as embryo national parks' directors, chief game wardens, tourist board directors (or senior assistants in these spheres) and other types of leading conservationists in their home countries.

There were sixty-three students on the course which ended mid-1969, divided into thirteen diploma and fifty certificate pupils. The countries they represented included Botswana, Zambia, Ghana, Cameroon, Ethiopia, Kenya and Uganda.

The minimum education requirement for entrance at Mweka is a Cambridge Overseas School Certificate or its equivalent. Candidates should have credits in biology, mathematics and English, the medium for all lectures.

Candidates have to undergo a rigorous medical examination to ensure they are physically fit for the course.

College fees of around £500 a year for each pupil cover tuition, uniforms of bush-jacket style, equipment, teaching material, lodging at Mweka, and materials for field work.

Governments and foreign benevolent organisations supporting individual students provide the fees which form the basis for operating the College's expenses. Financial support for development comes from external aid sources. Each student's sponsor also has to provide him with an allowance to cover messing and personal necessities.

The certificate course consists of basic instruction in the management of wild lands, and the diploma course provides a much more advanced level of training. Students who achieve a sufficiently high standard during the certificate course are selected for the Diploma Course. In both cases from one-third to half of the instruction time is spent on safari (Swahili for "Journey").

Classroom subjects cover botany, zoology, geology, an introduction to ecology, and natural history.

In the first instance, emphasis is on the collection and identification of plant species important to wild life.

A survey and classification of animals are made during the zoology studies, together with an appreciation of their evolution and geographical distribution. The zoology classes also embrace an introduction to life histories, anatomy, physiology and genetics —with emphasis on the vertebrates, particularly mammals.

Geology at the College covers various aspects of physical geology; the formation of rock, vulcanism, mountain formation, glaciation, weathering and erosion, and soil formation.

In ecology classes the students are shown the inter-relations among plants and animals and their environments. Concepts of populations, energy flow and nutrient cycles and ecosystems, and man's role in the biological community are also dealt with under this heading.

Studies are made in the natural history sessions of the breeding habits of game animals, their territories, movements, food and behaviour. The characteristic features of important species come under close review. The students are also taught identification of important and conspicuous bird species, especally game birds. Field trips are made for the study and identification of local forms, which are exotic and numerous.

General lessons on animal and range management deal with the application of ecological principles in

the control and use of wild animals. Expert lecturers
show how to determine and regulate the numbers and
species of animals which given habitats will support,
and how to sustain a yield for game cropping and
sports hunting.

The preservation of endangered species, factors
limiting game populations, and the management of
habitats for various conservation objectives are high
up on this section of the syllabus.

The course includes sufficient biometry to appreciate the problems of sampling animal populations.
Studies in forestry cover the importance of trees in
land-use planning, and the relations between forest
and game animals have to be examined and readily
identified by the students during their stay at the
college.

Range management tuition covers the principal
range plants and types of East Africa, principles of
plant physiology and ecology as related to game and
domestic grazing, techniques for measuring forage
and for determining range conditions and carrying
capacities. Elements of animal nutrition are examined.

Under "National Park Philosophy", the students
learn the principles of management and development
of such wild life strongholds, together with the
methods and techniques of communicating the value
of these protected areas to a wide, and generally
ignorant, public. For instance, many people throughout the world saw the controlled cropping of elephant
and hippo in one notoriously sensational film as an
example of African blood lust.

Practical and technical course work takes in
weapons training—the use, care and maintenance of
various types of firearms, with an emphasis on rifles.

This prepares the students for hunting dangerous animals attacking human habitations (a man needs a good deal of courage to seek out and destroy a marauding leopard or a rampaging, wounded buffalo in the bush), and for routine game control which is later carried out in the field.

Map reading and making, and compass work, are taught in advance of field expeditions, together with the operation and maintenance (embodying emergency repair work hundreds of miles from any garage) of Land-Rovers.

Students are taught the principles of collecting, preserving and exhibiting stuffed animal specimens in museums for educational purposes connected with game protection measures.

They have to swot up international conventions affecting wild life, the game policies of other countries in Africa and the outside world, and scores of examples of wild life legislation.

They study court procedures, with emphasis on the preparation and prosecution of cases against poachers and other violators of game laws.

They have to know the practical aspects of national park management such as budget estimates, accounting and reports, officer routine, stores and personal management, and supervision of transport.

Absorbing the lessons, beauties and perils of the wild lands the rugged way (in khaki shorts and shirts and bush-hats), the Mweka scholars apply their classroom instruction to the living fauna and flora.

Under the critical eyes of their teachers and away from the College for weeks at a time, they have to set tented camps in the bush at night after hacking out roads and trails.

The anti-poaching campaigns previously sketched out on blackboards become grim realities. Boundary marking and other forms of surveying have to be undertaken.

There are antelope to be captured by drug-darting for game ranching schemes which have been instituted by the College. Other animals are killed for the camp-fire pot, and to obtain their stomach contents and hides for research purposes.

The habits of the "Big Five"—elephant, rhino, lion, buffalo and leopard—have to be fully studied at close quarters! And students are encouraged to take up photography.

Each day they have to brave possible attacks by big game, and are prey to a host of deadly snakes. At nights there is but a stretch of green canvas between them and the terrifying cacophony all around.

Students participate in the preparation of game management plans and reports for use in the various areas, principally East Africa's game reserves which offer a variety of habitats, where studies are conducted.

Examinations are held at the College, itself located near the heart of some of the globe's finest game and vegetation areas, every six months, with a final, qualifying examination set at the end of the course.

One of the senior instructors at Mweka is leathery, gentle and genial Patrick Hemingway, middle-aged widower son of the late American author Ernest Hemingway's second wife. Pat, formerly a big-game hunter who has been on the staff of the College for several years, came to the green hills of Africa from Key West seventeen years ago.

"I am one of the few white men who got his job through Africanisation," he chuckled. "I like the work because the Africans who come to Mweka—drawn in increasing numbers by, perhaps, some deep-rooted sense of mission—are those who will save and nurture what is left of Africa's long-ravaged game populations.

"They have learned, and are anxious to use and pass on this knowledge, that the wild animals belong to the lasting beauty of Africa."

And the choice of calling reflects considerable credit upon their sincerity and self-sacrifice, for dawn-to-darkness game management and conservation work is relatively poorly paid, although men with an instinctive love and understanding of their broad, and often highly responsible, tasks are demanded.

So Hemingway spoke of his Mweka pupils, past and present, with admiration and affection.

"They have to walk on their own into the forest and count lion and elephant without a weapon of any sort," he told me in his lazy drawl as we sat on his verandah. "That takes a lot of guts on any man's part."

Pat's stock macabre joke—punctuated by a thunderous guffaw—is that he has never lost a student to a wild animal.

The remaining white instructors at Mweka—ex-game wardens or, like Hemingway, once professional hunters catering to visiting millionaires—are steadily being replaced by qualified Africans. The College will be all-black within the next four or five years, and a number of the instructors at the lectures and in the jungle will be men who learned their craft of practical mercy at Mweka.

By the end of 1970, Africa's second game management school, patterned on Mweka, will have been set up to serve the former French and British territories throughout West Africa. Before the doors were made, there were hundreds of applications for admission from a dozen countries on that half of the Continent.

Under the Black Star

Four years before he was overthrown as the leader of
Ghana by Army and police officers on February 24,
1966, Dr. Kwame Nkrumah had a grenade tossed at
him in a village near the border with Upper Volta.
Four people were killed, but Nkrumah escaped un-
hurt.

He said later that, as a result of this particular
assassination attempt, he had "lost a great deal of
faith in Man, the higher animal".

Seemingly to underline his contempt, Nkrumah
then gathered around him a variety of the "lower
beings", of the animal world, at Flagstaff House, his
official residence in the capital of Accra, which was
closely guarded by tanks and soldiers. In his extensive
and expensive private sanctuary were lions, guinea
pigs, leopards, turkeys, hippos, camels, hyenas, crocodiles, cobras, iguanas from Cuba, pythons, baboons,
Gaboon vipers, beavers from Canada, and puff
adders.

During the battle of Flagstaff House, on the day of
the coup (Nkrumah was in Peking) some of the President's pets were killed by mortar bombs and cannon
fire.

But, at the end of it all, most of the zoo and its occupants had been saved for the 9,000,000 people of Ghana. It costs about £1,000 a month to run, but every year thousands of adults and children pay their shillings and sixpences to see the animals there.

Early in 1969, a lioness and a leopard at Flagstaff House each gave birth to cubs under the care of the Head Keeper, 31-year-old Samuel K. Arthur, who has been in charge since Nkrumah set up the menagerie. The keeper is importing more animals from East Africa, a move which will be followed in a number of other West African countries anxious to re-start the breeding of certain wild species or to strengthen dwindling groups of others.

It is appropriate, perhaps, that Ghana is setting an example on the west side of the Continent in the rehabilitation of game populations. Land of cocoa and gold which in the slaving days was known as the "Gold Coast", Ghana was the first British Colony in Africa to win its freedom—on March 6, 1957.

Ghana—its impressive national flag consists of three horizontal bars of red, gold and green with a black star in the middle of the gold—is 350 miles wide and 400 miles in length. It lies almost in the centre of the countries along the Gulf of Guinea, and is a few degrees north of the Equator.

It is bordered by the French-speaking countries of Togo, Upper Volta and the Ivory Coast, and consists of three geographical zones—the northern savannahs, the forest lands, and a flat coastal belt washed by Atlantic rollers and dotted with crumbling, white-walled slave forts. The country—once known as "The White Man's Grave"—has a tropical climate which is largely influenced both by the hot, dry and dust-laden black *harmattan* blowing from the Sahara and

Dr. Kenneth Kaunda, President of Zambia.

Ranger force heading for the bush in Tanzania's Serengeti National Park.

Zebra in the Serengeti National Park, Tanzania.

the cool, wet trade winds coming in from across the ocean.

In the north, farmers grow maize or raise cattle on the open country. The rolling hills of the central and western parts of Ghana are covered by cocoa farms, the country's mainstay, and heavy timber trees.

The rainy season is from May to September, and the dry season from October to March or April.

Ghana is trisected by the Volta River and its two tributaries, the Black and White Voltas. A fourteenth of Ghana's land area is covered by the great Volta Lake, created by the dam built for hydro-electric power at Akosombo in the south-east.

Her rulers concede that Ghana, so virile and progressive in other respects, has in the troubled past lagged behind much of East Africa in game preservation policies. But there is these days considerable evidence, in personnel and programmes, of a growing awareness of the valuable part wild animals can play in the national scheme of things.

Ghana's principal and best-known game reserve—Mole in the Damongo district—has just been increased in area from 900 to 1,620 square miles.

Established twelve years ago in the north-west, 420 miles from Accra, the Mole reserve (watered by the river of that name) rises in some parts to 1,000 feet above sea level. The majority of the West African savannah animals live there, such as oribi, bushbuck, the Western hartebeest, crown duiker, the red-flanked duiker, warthog, baboon, waterbuck, green monkey, Roan antelope, reedbuck and bush pig. In lesser degrees, there are also elephant, lion, crocodiles, leopard and monitor lizards. More than 200 species of birds, including the European varieties which migrate during the dry season, have been recorded there.

c

The Goaso game reserve in the south, staffed by African game scouts, contains elephant, buffalo, Bongo and a variety of other animals.

Kujani, on the shore of Lake Volta, is the home of, among others, buffalo, hippo, elephant and waterbuck.

The smaller Shai Hills reserve, 35 miles east of Accra and covering 23 square miles, harbours chiefly plains game.

Few people can remember ever seeing a rhinoceros in Ghana, and cheetah families may have to be reintroduced to the country.

At the spearhead of modern conservation measures in Ghana are men like Christopher Manu who was born into a tribal clan of twenty on a fifty-square-mile cocoa plantation near Kumasi in 1940. Christopher helped with the gathering of cocoa beans until the age of eight. He was then admitted to a Catholic mission school, a day primary.

Two years later, his father died and the boy's mother took him back with her to her home village.

Christopher Manu learned a great deal about the haunts and habits of wild animals, and how to ensure his own survival, from the tender age of ten.

Every evening or early morning, the boy would go out into the forest alone, to collect the nuts of the kola tree from the ground to pay his school fees and help feed his family. The nuts, used in preparations either as a tonic, a condiment or an antidote to alcohol, fetched a penny or so each from middlemen.

Like so many Africans of his calibre in animal conservation work, Mr. Manu is truly a self-made man who was born in poverty and has made his way up a steep and overcrowded ladder by sheer industry and personal sacrifice.

After seven years of gleaning nuts and learning the three Rs, he won a scholarship to a secondary school in Kumasi, and there, for another seven years, he studied biology, mathematics, Latin and physics, and subsequently also botany, zoology and chemistry as a preparatory course for the University of Ghana.

At the University he chose bio-chemistry and zoology, specialising in marine biology, as his subjects.

From 1965 to 1966 he was employed—for his subsequent BSc (Honours) degree—as a research officer with the Ghana Government's progressive Fisheries Department. Earlier, he had worked for the Game Department for a short period as part of his university course so, when he had obtained his degree, he decided to switch from marine biology "to give a helping hand to a friend who was a fully qualified wild life management officer".

The "helping hand" lasted two years. He was made an assistant game warden, and initially, in the north, he had to undertake field research on the distribution and movements of game like the dwarf buffalo, leopards, elephant, and the black duiker.

"Another of my jobs later was to persuade poachers to give up their way of life and become maize or yam farmers in the area. It was generally the lazy people who did not want the hard work of farming who became poachers, using steel traps and muzzle-loaders to get game meat for the markets. Killing for ivory was only a rare sideline with them.

"When these illegal hunters saw how successful the law-abiding could become on agricultural land, or I was able to convince them of this, many gave up and

joined the farmers. So the poaching problem up there
reduced itself."

Fines of up to £100, or six months' imprisonment,
are the basic penalties for poaching in Ghana.

"As a rule, our first checks on poachers are made
in the markets which are such a crowded and dazzling
a feature of rural and urban life in West Africa,"
said Mr. Manu. "In 1967, I followed an elephant
poacher from a market, all along his trails, until I
caught him deep in the bush. I was out of uniform
and wandering around the market-place when I
heard the women gossiping about an elephant which
had been kill up-country the day before.

"The poacher, I learned, was a man who used a
double-barrel shotgun to fire arrows which, as in
Serengeti and some other parts of Africa, had poison
smeared on the shafts just behind the head. We had
been looking for him for some time. He did not kill
quickly and cleanly every elephant he stalked. Then
the wounded beast would go on a rampage, menacing
villages and breaking up herds. We *had* to bring this
man to book."

For the first fifteen miles, Mr. Manu, unarmed,
followed the culprit's tracks in a Land-Rover. He was
to march all day in the jungle for nineteen miles before he finally caught up with his quarry.

"I left the Land-Rover at the side of a track, and struck
out into the trees. After several hours, desperately thirsty
in the intense heat and with my clothes clinging soggily
to me, I came upon a village and the people crowded
round me in curiosity.

"I asked about my man, without revealing I wanted
to arrest him for poaching. I described him with signs
and gestures, and pretended I had been sent to summon
him to appear before the Paramount Chief. This was

an order he would probably dare not disobey; and, in any case, the villagers were bound to assist me in carrying it out.

"Some of their warriors took me a few more miles to a forest clearing where there were the carcasses of three elephant, in a fog of flies, which the poacher had slaughtered.

"We found him close to the scene of the crime and, with the young guides obliged to protect me in my assumed role as the chief's emissary, I was able to take the man into custody without him making more than a token show of resistance."

Under questioning at police headquarters, the poacher claimed he had been given a licence to kill two elephants and was attacked by a third while shooting the others. "I had to kill it to save my life," he pleaded.

Licence or no licence, he had no authority to use poisoned arrows in a gun. He was tried, therefore, on a technical charge of "using a dangerous weapon"— as his ingenious lethal instrument certainly was   and fined £50. He promised to reform.

"He probably became a game scout," said Mr. Manu. "Quite a few of these fellows are ex-poachers who know all the ropes. It doesn't take *them* long to nab the bad men."

In July, 1968, Mr. Manu went to America on concentrated courses related to game conservation and the running of national parks. At the end of these studies, in September of the same year, he was chosen by the Food and Agricultural Organisation of the United Nations to go to the College of African Wildlife Management in Tanzania as a teacher of natural history.

It was a signal honour for he became the College's

first African lecturer, the initial link between the past
and the future at Mweka.

When we talked there in mid-1969 he was preparing to make a tour of game parks all over Africa before returning to Ghana to be in the forefront of its
conservation development schemes.

His white colleagues at the College lauded Chris
Manu's talents, and the African pupils obviously
found inspiration in the hard-won successes of a
career still unfolding.

Mr. Manu used to sit in at lectures at the College
on advanced subjects, and enjoyed being "a teacher
who's gone back to the school-desk". And, whenever
the opportunity arose, he would spend weeks or days
out on safari with newly-enrolled students.

"There's always something new to learn about
animals and their ways, some new adventure to experience in the bush," he added. "And when I'm back
in harness in Ghana—what with tourist promotion
tailored to those huge planes—there will be youngsters to train as tomorrow's guardians of the game
tracts. And, maybe, there will be new reserves to mark
out on the maps."

He smiled gently with deep gratification at the
thought.

Abuko

The Gambia, a brightly patterned "python" of West African land and river which—independent since February, 1965—snakes 300 miles into French-speaking Senegal, was Britain's smallest (4,000 square miles) and oldest African possession.

Groundnuts, stacked high on the decks of leisurely sailing cutters, form the mainstay of a flimsy economy for 400,000 elegantly costumed, poor but carefree, people—with profitable sidelines provided by sun-seeking tourists fleeing the European winter months, and the gentle smuggling of English cigarettes, fabrics and bicycles into Senegal.

Although, like Kenya, it has large and varied numbers of uncommon and richly plumaged birds, the Gambia has practically no big game running completely wild.

Exceptionally large specimens of wild pig are common in some low-lying areas, and hippo and crocodile can be seen in other parts together with lively dog-faced baboons.

Species that live in the Gambia River and on its wooded banks are best viewed on a five-day trip up-

19

or down-stream in a steamer of the larger "African
Queen" class which carries passengers, cargo—and a
post office.

Most of the amiable Gambians are law-abiding
folk (apart from that sporting degree of "honest smuggling"), but now and then an unscrupulous fisherman
in his vividly painted, square-sailed canoe will net or
harpoon a manatee (the West African name for
the dugong, or sea cow) off the Atlantic shore and
offer succulent steaks from it for sale in the local
market.

Both stall-owners and fishermen have been warned
by official proclamations in Bathurst, the seaside capital, that anyone caught killing or selling a manatee,
which is "absolutely protected" by the laws of the
Gambia, will be prosecuted.

The latest edict, issued early in 1969, reminded
the public that other protected species in the country
include the West African eland (*jinki-janko*), the situtunga (*sio wulleng*), and elephant (*samo*). And a
widely circulated notice issued by the Gambian Ministry of Agriculture and Natural Resources at about
the same time drew attention to the Cruelty to Animals Act which provides for six months' hard labour
and a fine of £25 for "keeping animals under conditions constituting cruelty". The red light in this
instance was directed at the hawkers of baby chimpanzees and other small animals. The Government is
determined to put these stony-hearted, illegal traders
out of business.

One of the reasons for the scarcity of game animals
at large in the Gambia is that over the years several
species have been forced to withdraw to the larger,
less populated areas of surrounding Senegal which

also boasts lion, elephant and buffalo in one
big national park containing 300 miles of tracks
alone.

The Gambia is getting back a number of her once
indigenous animals from Senegal, and at the same
time is providing protection for the survivors of her
species, and making additions to them.

A 200-acre nature reserve named Abuko, the first
of its kind in this little country from which Mungo
Park, the explorer, set out on his West African travels,
came modestly into being recently, and its pace
crippled by lack of funds from an all-but-bare
Treasury—has since been slowly, but efficiently, developed.

Abuko began by being surrounded by a six-foot
high, chain-link fence. It became rusty in parts, holes
had to be "patched" with wire, and later it was stif-
fened along its entire length where necessary with
timber posts donated by a prominent well-wisher, the
American Ambassador in Senegal's capital of
Dakar.

Some of the early damage to the perimeter fence
was caused by the owners of pigs and goats propping
up the bottom of the fencing or scooping out the earth
below it to take their animals inside the reserve to
graze. Time and again, the wilful trespassers were
accosted and driven away.

A forty-foot wide, roughly graded fire-trace was
cut round the entire reserve inside the perimeter fence.
This performs the dual purpose of protection from
bush fires outside Abuko, and as a route for Land-
Rovers and maintenance vehicles used by the staff to
make spot checks for poachers, fence repairs, and
fire inspections.

The long-term intention is to consolidate the perimeter fence with a live fence of hedges (bearing both
sharp thorns and seed pods rich in protein and palatable to game) and rhum palms. The lofty palms will
make Abuko clearly visible for miles, both from the
air and ground level.

Despite the critical and constant shortage of money,
measures to securely fence the reserve are always
given priority to obviate as far as possible the danger
of animals being lured out through gaps to their
deaths by poachers with baits and decoys.

In Abuko all flora and fauna—animals, reptiles,
birds, trees, bushes, shrubs and flowers—are safeguarded.

A pioneer scatter-sowing programme with the seed
of a number of the Gambia's national trees has been
carried out in the reserve, but the effect will not be
apparent for a number of years.

On this, an official of the Government of the
Gambia reported: "It is a start, however, towards
repairing the ravages of the tree flora that had taken
place (before the creation of the reserve), and will
result in the introduction of a number of new species
with which further charm and interest may be added
to Abuko. These sowings and plantings will continue
annually with the aim in view of establishing a fairly
representative collection of our main trees and the
more colourful shrubs. The main emphasis, however,
will always be on maintaining the natural charm of
the reserve, and all introduction will be most carefully
considered in order to avoid any suggestion of con-
trived effect."

The original specimens donated by their African
owners in the Gambia for release in Abuko consisted
of two jackal cubs, six porcupines, three Royal

pythons, two monkeys and a pair of parrots. Crocodile were already there, in a lake pool.

In June of 1969 the population in the reserve also included Gambian sun squirrels; leopard; three West African chimpanzees (the only ones then in the Gambia, and put in Abuko to breed); Nile monitor lizards, including one measuring six feet long; red Colobus monkeys and green vervet monkeys; serval and genet cats; the West African civet; the spotted palm civet; bushbuck; West African moles; antelope; the Gambian dwarf mongoose, and two types of porcupine, the Bush-Tailed and the Great Crested.

And Senegal promised to return to Gambia for the reserve a selection of buck and antelope such as oribi, waterbuck, reedbuck and Maxwell's duiker.

An attractive rest-house for game-viewing in comfort has been built half-way round Abuko's circular route from collections among parties of tourists from abroad after lectures and slide shows on the Gambia's natural history.

Ornamental planting, with trees and exotic shrubs, has taken place in the immediate environs of this rest-house, but it is one of the few places in the reserve where the hand of Man is obvious.

Botanical specimens are being sent from the reserve for classification to Britain and America.

It has stimulated natural history studies at all levels in the Gambia and led to regular educational visits by groups of school children.

Cramped as Abuko is, it has found space within its boundaries for an animal orphanage—"a large enclosure wherein animals that have been found, very young, in the bush and raised by hand, or the unwanted pets of people, may be released in reasonable safety . . . and which facilitates visitors' photographs of a far more intimate nature than might otherwise be possible."

Orphanages, such as in Kenya and the Gambia, give the animals a far greater degree of safe freedom than would otherwise be possible while enabling them to live to a large extent fairly naturally.

"Nothing could be better suited for conveying to visitors the need for, and the absolute desirability of, Nature conservation," states a Gambian governmental report on Abuko, "than for those visitors to be able to mix with creatures at close quarters in their natural surroundings and to see for themselves the character and beauty of some of the animals that mankind in its headlong rush for 'progress' seems bent upon destroying."

The Republic of Nigeria, which was stricken for thirty months by the bloodiest civil war in Africa's history, has a population of around 60,000,000 and is four times the size of Great Britain, or equal to the combined American States of Texas, Alabama, Indiana and Delaware.

A Government handbook for visitors states with melancholy candour: "Big game of the species usually associated with Africa is not plentiful at present in Nigeria." Active measures, it is stated, have been taken to establish game reserves "where such animals can flourish and be seen".

The first of these was set up at Yankari in north-eastern Nigeria, covering 72 square miles of woodland and savannah and including the sites of a number of villages which were abandoned because of slave-raiding and inter-tribal wars a century ago.

Yankari is open to tourists from December to the middle of each following year. There is a central camp of buildings and tents at Wikki warm springs where Neolithic Age implements have been found.

Throughout the dry season, the game is concentrated in the neighbourhood of the central Gaji river, and the animals are seen in the greatest numbers in the early mornings and the late afternoons when they come in to drink.

The Yankari Reserve is not open during the wet season because of difficulty of access, the animals are difficult to observe because of the tall grass, and many species breed during the rains and should be left undisturbed.

The Nigerian Army has helped to build bridges and roads in Yankari where the uniformed, be-fezzed game scouts—ex-hunters with an intimate knowledge of the locality—act as guides to visitors, and the game guards are ex-soldiers or former policemen.

Reptiles in Yankari include the Nile crocodile and the Royal python, while birds range from the sacred ibis to the black-bellied bustard.

Elephant, buffalo, bushbuck, hunting dogs, two species of duiker, the Western hartebeest, waterbuck, hippo, ground squirrels, oribi and monkeys are resident in, or regular visitors to the reserve. Giraffe, cheetah, leopard, the spotted hyena and lion are rarely seen.

Most of the giraffe remaining in West Africa are in national parks and game reserves, and even in these protected areas their numbers are small. In Nigeria as a whole, where giraffe were fairly numerous seventy years ago, there are now hardly any at all. Herds remain in Cameroon, the Central African Republic, Mali, Senegal and Chad. But giraffe are conspicuous by their absence in Dahomey, Ghana, Guinea, Ivory Coast, Liberia, Togo, Upper Volta and southern Nigeria.

Elephant have been gravely reduced in some parts of West Africa by the shooting out of those which were said to have trampled and ruined crops, or threatened people. Executors will be less arbitrary in future.

An East African ecologist who knows Nigeria well said in Kenya that he had returned to the south of the country in 1969 to carry out a foot safari in an area which before the civil war ("when killing man became a priority") supported large numbers of wild animals.

"Every night," he said, "there was dead silence. Not even the whirr of a grasshopper. It was the most eerie thing I have ever experienced."

Yet all game in Nigeria is protected under the Wild Animals Preservation Law—in times of peace, at least.

In the northern regions of the country, concern with internecine conflict had not remained so intense as in the lower half of Nigeria, so other game reserves, apart from Yankari, were created or considered even before peace was restored. And wild animals in variety and relatively large numbers can still be seen around Lake Chad which is bounded by Nigeria, troubled Chad and Niger.

An official, coloured map of the latter country shows districts, mainly in the southern half, inhabited by elephant, rhino, lion, giraffe, antelope and various types of monkey, and it maintains zoological gardens with lion, hippo, hyenas, giraffe, gazelles, ostriches, and crocodiles.

Cameroon expects a record 36,000 tourists in 1970, the chief attraction for them being the well-administered Waza National Park in the north which is flanked by the Kapsikis Mountains. There are several safari camps within this extensive reserve where thousands of giraffe, so scarce elsewhere in West Africa, are to be seen in the course of a day's drive.

The Government of Sierra Leone has announced it welcomes external investment for the development of tourism and the setting up of a game reserve. (How well I recall the wonder and excitement of our African taxi-driver there when a dappled fawn skittered across the lonely coastal road in front of our car a dozen miles out of Freetown). A number of areas are being constituted game reserves (and some existing forest Reserves given that increased status) under Sierra Leone's wild life conservation measures.

Special funds, which could not be voted previously in earlier years owing to financial and political difficulties, have been earmarked for these schemes by the Government which "now considers wild life as a national asset that must be wisely used and developed for tourism purposes". A Game Superintendent has been recruited for training in Tanzania.

Elephant, hippo, the bush cow, crocodile, chimpanzees, and various kinds of antelope and monkey are among the animals to be fostered in Sierra Leone.

Meanwhile, gallant Gambia—struggling to exist, literally, on peanuts—is a speck of gold on the West

African game salvation scene. And Abuko stands, as one admirer so soberly described it, as "a development of merit and foresight". It is equally an example and a rebuke to several of the Gambia's big brother States.

Snares and hacked-up victims found in a poachers' camp in Serengeti National Park, Tanzania.

Loomis Dean of Life *Magazine*

A poacher's grass hut set ablaze by African game rangers during a swoop in Northern Tanzania.

Loomis Dean of Life *Magazine*

Loading poached ivory aboard a dug-out canoe in a lonely creek on the East African coast. The ivory was later smuggled on to dhows anchored offshore, and taken to the Middle East where it was sold illegally.

Giraffe and zebra together form bizarre patterns—in the Masai Mara Game Reserve.

Marion Kaplan

Field force arresting poachers in Tsavo National Park, Kenya.

Marion Kaplan

Woebegone poacher, under arrest.

Marion Kaplan

Field force take prisoners with illegal trophies back to headquarters.

Hugo the Hippo

Whenever snide stories are told by former white settlers of the black man's indifference to the fate of animals, I think of Hugo.

Hugo is a hippopotamus who aroused the abiding compassion of an African country the size of Spain and Portugal and half of France rolled into one.

Never before in the history of wild life conservation in Tanzania—where the wild animal population is one of the greatest in the world and is said to outnumber the human population of 13,000,000—has a single beast caused such concern as Hugo. He is reputed to be the only one of his kind living in salt water. But that alone is not his claim to wide fame. . . .

In a bygone age, the Sultan of the clove island of Zanzibar decided that Kuransini creek on the mainland opposite his domain should be kept free of sharks so that he and his court could bathe without peril in this quiet water off a lagoon which is now Dar-es-Salaam's busy harbour. To this end, he had a family of hippo driven down river into the creek where they made their home.

During colonial times, however, the guardians of

Kurasini were declared vermin, and eight of them were destroyed. By 1960, so the stories go, there were only three hippos left—"King George" (given this title by the locals because of his plumpness), a female and their son who is now known as Hugo.

He was but a five-hundredweight stripling, six months old, when both his parents were shot and killed by white men. The baby hippo managed to escape into the reeds on shore.

The ungainly orphan quickly learned to live on his wits. He became docile, then playful, in the sea-salt reaches of the creek. Years after the tragedy of his parents—with Tanzania a free state—he was a two-ton rival in attraction to Kenya's Elsa, the "Born Free" lioness.

At low tide Hugo could be seen splashing around in the Indian Ocean, or performing graceful ballets under the waves in the clear water at the entrance to the creek. Water-skiers towed behind speed-boats skimmed harmlessly over his partly submerged, shiny-black back. He followed yachts and swimmers, sported with dogs, and became a firm friend of the African fishermen in their lateen-sail canoes, who claimed that not only did he scare off sharks but attracted shoals of curious fish. Ashore, he marched behind herds of cattle. Children lost all fear of him. People flocked to Kurasini, which covers five miles of water, to see the lone, but happy, hippo.

There are two versions of how he got his name. One is that he was given it by a reporter on the local paper (recounting some of Hugo's first exploits) after a sub-editor had rejected the name "Horatio" because it would not have fitted a single-column head-line. The other is that when visitors asked to see the hippo in the grey-green waters of the palm-fringed

creek on the outskirts of Dar-es-Salaam, the local
Africans would point out a sand-bank on which he
usually rested, saying "huko" in Swahili, meaning
"there". Tourists mistook this to mean his name was
"Hugo".

Kurasini provides ample grass to feed on, but during the high summer of 1965 it became so badly
scorched and inedible that hunger forced him into the
small-holdings on the banks of a dozen peasant
farmers. Everyone still loved Hugo—except those few
victims of his pangs.

The amiable juggernaut, leaving behind foot-
prints the size of soup plates, nightly strolled a few
hundred yards up the yellow slopes, through the tall
papyrus, to gargantuan meals of sweet potatoes,
plump cabbages, lettuces, cassava roots and maize
cobs; rice paddies in his path were badly damaged;
flower gardens uprooted.

Like his fellows, Hugo can move at speeds of up to
30 miles an hour on land despite a huge bulk and,
with excellent hearing and eyesight and hair-trigger
instincts of self-preservation born of his early days,
he regularly evaded his farmer pursuers—"He goes
like a galloping horse," said one—who were re-
peatedly aroused in the middle of the night by his
blissful snortings among their crops.

Back in the creek at dawn after every rampage,
Hugo stood defiantly on his sand-bank and gave a
prodigious hippo's "laugh" to the enraged tribesmen
and their families who lined the shore with spears
and muzzle-loaders impotently in their hands, their
ravaged patches of land behind them.

For all his evasive skill and cunning, it seemed it
would be but a matter of time before Hugo was ambushed by the farmers and received a charge of buck-

shot in his brain or was hacked to death with sharp-bladed *pangas*.

It was then that the massive "Save Hugo" campaign, supported by the general public, African game wardens and rangers, schoolchildren, the Tanzania Society for the Prevention of Cruelty to Animals, visiting animal lovers and later the President himself, got under way.

To save him from himself, thunderflashes were used to drive the hippo back into the water at night. Hugo, now something of a gourmet, kept on coming.

A woman living in Dar, who once raised dollars to buy rubber bootees for cobble-sore Moroccan donkeys, collected £150 to create a Kurasini sanctuary for Hugo where other animals, "preferably orphans", she stipulated, could join him and "live free from fear, want or suffering".

The Kurasini small-holders, busily replanting, retorted: "The best treatment for Hugo is a bullet through his head. The Government will get his teeth for ivory, the people will enjoy a tasty stew, and the money collected on his behalf can be donated to a charity."

Receiving scant sympathy in official quarters, they were advised to fence their properties.

The T.S.P.C.A., late in 1965, launched its fund to help Hugo change his address, and to remove the threat of sudden death. The idea—once he was caught —was to transport him to a tranquil hippo lake in the Mikumi National Park, 160 miles from Kurasini. An African schoolgirl, among a multitude of contributors, mailed three weeks' pocket money of sixpence to the Society.

African Boy Scouts devised a "Hugo Dance" which

they performed in circles, imitating the hippo's pon-
derous gait—with a great deal of stamping and shuff-
ling and occasional loud bellows.

Children in classes brought Hugo into their morning prayers, and throughout the land sang a rough,
newly-composed ditty of praise to him in Swahili:

> "The hippo's name is Hugo,
> He lives in Hippo Bay,
> In lovely Kurasini,
> He is so tame and gay,
> He does not need finances,
> He does not smoke or drink,
> He only needs his chances,
> To stay alive and sing,
> 'My friends are all the people,
> Scouts and T.S.P.C.A.
> I'm in Kurasini to stay!'.
> Hugo, Hugo, Hugo."

An African headmaster wrote a textbook in Swahili
for Tanzanian primary schools. His subject: Hugo
the Hippo.

President Nyerere ordered that all efforts were to
be made to save Hugo. A gang of convicts from the
local prison were put to work at the creekside. Across
a dinner trail used by Hugo, marked by trampled
grass and bare bushes, they dug a pit, several feet
deep. The Game Department then took over. Rangers
built a tall, log and banana-leaf hide, with a wooden
platform, about four yards from the pit into which
they lowered a stout wooden crate, nine feet long and
six feet wide. The open top of this had been spread
with branches—on which three succulent pumpkins
were the bait.

The plan, we were told at the spot, was that when
Hugo stumbled into the trap on one of his nocturnal

forays the two rangers stationed in the hide would leap down from the platform, manhandle the lid of the crate over to the pit, and slam it down on top of the dangerously infuriated captive.

Hugo was then to be hauled out in his crate by a mobile crane, and taken off to Mikumi by way of a triumphal drive, befitting a national hero, through the streets of Dar in an open truck, escorted by white-helmeted motor-cycle policemen and cheered by tens of thousands of African fans lining the route.

But Hugo shunned this scheme, and the promised honours. For scores of long, weary nights, the game rangers kept a fruitless vigil. Then, at last, Hugo appeared on the scene. In the blackness, he could be heard approaching the trap, and the African watchers crouched for instant action. Hugo's sniffings were like the gusts of a gale.

Then he turned away suddenly at the lip of the pit, crashed through the tangled undergrowth and was never detected at that spot again.

By now Hugo had become a world figure. He was written about in newspapers in Russia, Austria, Czechoslovakia, and Germany. He was featured on television in Britain and America. They were mainly shots with telephoto lenses, for Hugo, perhaps remembering the killing of his mother and father, hated anything that looked like a gun pointing at him from close range. *Time* magazine made much of Hugo. In June, 1966 the magazine described him as "Tanzania's favourite hippo . . . the talk of the whole country."

The African executive director of the T.S.P.C.A. pointed out that, in the efforts to spare Hugo, a "so-called under-developed country" was "leading the field in humanity". Where one hippo more or less might not count in a large population of behemoths, the people, he said, found it important to save the life of a single specimen.

Meanwhile, crafty Hugo—ignorant of the V.I.P. fête that awaited him—had moved to another part of the creek and continued to defy all attempts to capture him.

He loved music (especially rousing marches), but amplified renderings of Sousa—and even the "Indian Love Call" from "Rose Marie"—failed to lure him out of hiding.

He spurned green leaves and buckets of water placed near his haunts to deter him from raiding the crop-growing *shambas*.

Hugo, it was said, had gone coy after getting a scare from the strong scent of rangers who had waited to box him up.

The original blind was finally dismantled, and game rangers searched for fresh shore trails of Hugo's leading up from the deep pools where he remained, below the surface for long intervals, as if sulking.

Prisoners in broad arrow uniforms dug new pits. In each case there was the hypothetical problem of how to get a truck and a big enough crane across the fine sand and through a miniature jungle to the pit into which he might tumble. Game trappers said darts containing a tranquilliser drug would have to be fired into Hugo's thick flanks from a crossbow or a rifle to quieten his fearsome thrashings before he could be hauled out of the pit in leather-bound steel slings. Other experts maintained this would be too dangerous—for Hugo.

One of the original Hugo crusaders urged the erection of a fence of stout stakes around a plot of land on the bank of the Kurasini to give him a playground-

larder opposite the pool in which he had last been
seen.

Rangers at one of the freshly-dug pits reported
Hugo's reappearance from the water. It seemed that,
at last, curiosity might lead to his (literal) downfall.
On two consecutive nights, however, he merely snuf-
fled around the leading end of the pit along the trail,
ignoring the bales of fresh grass spread around and,
snout in the air, made his way back to his old snort-
ing grounds at the edge of the creek.

Tanzania's only white Cabinet Minister, Mr. Derek
Bryceson, responsible for wild life, forestry and agriculture, joined the ranks of Hugo's would-be saviours
and announced he was considering calling on Dr.
Bernhard Grzimek, world-famous German zoologist
and author of *Serengeti Shall Not Die* who says game
conservation may be one of the main contributions of
black nations to the civilisation of mankind, to direct
rescue work on his next visit to Tanzania.

The T.S.P.C.A. acknowledged that more than
twenty soft traps had been laid for Hugo, but he
had not put a foot near one of them. Said an official
of the Society: "Obviously, he has no intention of
leaving his seaside home for the unknown, inland
world on Mikumi."

The families with plots renewed their clamour for
an end to Hugo. Pleading they had inadequate
weapons to execute him, they asked the Game Department to gun him down with heavy-calibre bullets.
But, at the behest of the President, the Government
sharp-shooters continued to stay their hand.

For a long time now there has been no complaint
against Hugo from the farmers, and it seems he no
longer seeks the delicacies of civilisation. And the soils
of Kurasini are becoming exhausted. Under Presi-

dent Nyerere's Arusha Declaration of robust social-
ism, peasants have been exhorted to work collectively
over large areas to increase production, and the Kurasini folk will have no alternative but to move away
to more fertile land.

So the handful of Hugo's earstwhile enemies have
become friends who appear reluctant to take their
leave of the creek in which his peace and safety now
seems assured.

Tears for Crocodiles

There are few African villages that do not retain the tragic memory of some member of the tribe—a woman washing clothes on the mottled stones in midstream, a wandering toddler or, perhaps, a herdsman swimming with his steers—being seized by a crocodile and dragged to its underwater fœtid larder, never to be seen again.

Such ghastly incidents are on a sharp decline—but only because the crocodile populations of Africa (long over-hunted, and hounded by poachers, as skins from seven to nine feet long today fetch from £15 to £20 each) have been reduced to numbers verging on disappearance. And it is the Africans—with less cause than anybody to care for these blood-chilling reptiles with their evil smirk and cold, unblinking eyes (they do *not* weep when devouring their prey)—who are fighting to save the scaly monsters that would seem least likely to need any form of protection.

However, the skin of the crocodile, like that of the leopard, continues to have a high market value in the world of fashion, being used, particularly in Britain, France and America, to make—from the belly sections—shoes, handbags, belts and expensively ugly baubles of the souvenir trade.

In the peak years of the middle forties, European hunters in then British-administered Uganda were killing around 13,000 crocodiles a year. Such uncontrolled carnage led to the extermination of crocodile colonies in Lake Kioga and stretches of Lake Victoria.

The only sizeable populations now left are in Uganda's national parks, and, as in Murchison Falls, these are still being heavily preyed upon.

"The greatest caution must be exercised at all times in approaching the water's edge, for death in a ghastly form may be lurking anywhere unseen," states the guide book to Murchison Falls National Park where hundreds of crocodiles basking on the sand-banks of the Nile are the chief wild life attraction.

This warning does nothing to deter the poachers and, in fact, it is now the Victoria Nile crocodiles themselves that are facing a gory end, and at some places where they were moving into the river within the park there are at present none at all.

In the last two decades the Nile crocodile alone has been subjected to so much indiscriminate exploitation that in 1970 it is an endangered or extinct species in many parts of Africa.

The Murchison Falls National Park supports the last relatively large population in Uganda and, with the disappearance of crocodiles elsewhere, it assumes an increasing value both as a reservoir of the species and as a rare spectacle for tourists.

The latest official report on Uganda's crocodiles declares: "The change that has taken place on both banks of the Nile below Paraa, where formerly crocodiles abounded, is most striking." In 1952 one of the most spectacular congregations to be found anywhere

on the Victoria Nile was the Mugungu grounds.
There one could see a compact formation of reptiles
so numerous that when disturbed it looked as though
the whole beach was moving into the river. This con-
gregation was still present in strength in 1957. Four
years later the place was deserted, and in 1967 an
aerial survey over the sector of the Nile revealed only
two crocodiles between Paraa and Lake Albert. The
nesting population below Paraa has been virtually
exterminated by skin hunters."

The report continues:

"In 1961 the low 300 yards of the sand river on the north
bank, in the gorge below the Falls (where the Nile thun-
ders through 'the eye of a needle'), was occupied by undisturbed breeding crocodiles. In 1967 the craters of some
nine excavated nests were found near the river mouth.
In 1968 the sand river had no nests at all. At one place
on the south bank, in 1967, there were thirteen excava-
tions of hatched or raided nests. In 1968 only one nest
was found, and this was destroyed by monitors (large
dragon-like lizards).

"Two counts carried out by a Fisheries officer in 1967
revealed a population of about 420 crocodiles between
Paraa ferry and Murchison Falls. An aerial count the
same year put the population at not less than 700. In
April, 1968, an air survey by the Chief Warden gave a
total of 534 crocodiles in the sector. During the first four
months of 1968, which covered the whole incubation
period, a detailed survey of breeding females was made
between Paraa and the Falls. Some 181 nests were found.
Allowing for a small percentage that escaped detection,
it is estimated that the total number of nesting females
is now (early 1969) certainly below 250.

"Destruction by poachers is undoubtedly the most important factor in this decline. The park's crocodiles have
been reduced to a fraction of their former numbers. Losses

are believed to average about twenty skins a month. A
population that carries not more than 250 nesting females
cannot sustain such losses for long."

The tourists and Nature came in for their share of
the blame in the report.

"Recent observations and experiments have clearly
shown the vital part played by maternal care in the successful rearing of young crocodiles. If the females are
unable, through human disturbance, to carry out their
proper functions, eggs and hatchlings perish. Crocodiles
have a well defined breeding season. In the Murchison
reach of the Victoria Nile mating takes place in December, most eggs are laid by mid-January, and hatching
occurs in late March and early April. During the three-
month incubation period, the female remains in attendance, either lying over the eggs or watching the nest from
nearby cover, actively defending it from predatory egg-
eaters. Her presence is necessary for the survival of the
clutch."

And it seems the much maligned monsters have
tender skins to their reptilian natures. They call—by
croaking forlornly—to their mothers as they break
out of their eggs, and she comes quickly to clear away
the firmly compacted earth with her claws. No hatching could take place without her aid.

Immediately after hatching the young seek the
shelter of their parent's body, and they are led or con-
veyed by her to a selected nursery site in slack, shallow water with protective vegetable cover. In the
absence of the parent, the hatchlings tend to remain
near the nest where they fall an easy prey to enemies.
Having reached the water, they become strongly
gregarious, and school together in the nursery for at
least six weeks. During this critical period of early life
the female closely attends her offspring. Without such

after-care they are defenceless against attacks from
Goliath herons, marabou storks, fish eagles, kites and
other predators.

"Thus, during the protracted cycle of egg-laying, incubation, exhumation, hatching and the first weeks of active
life the eggs and young are entirely dependent upon
maternal care. Disturbance of females on the nesting
grounds causes high mortality, both through hatching
failure and predation. Protection from interference during
the successive phases of the reproductive cycle is therefore absolutely necessary for the long term survival of
the population.

"But the peak tourist season coincides with the crocodile breeding season, and it is common practice for
launches to run alongside the more accessible basking and
breeding grounds. Crocodiles that have not already fled
to the water are then driven off for the edification of the
tourists. They may suffer this interference a dozen times
a day. The spectacle of monitors and baboons excavating
crocodile eggs provides additional entertainment for
visitors.

"Losses due to predation on both eggs and hatchlings
are very high. In the main this is a secondary effect of
the human disturbance by poachers and launch-parties.
In 1968, of 174 nests whose history is known no fewer
than 97 (55·7%) clutches of eggs were entirely destroyed
by egg-eating enemies, and 29 (16·7%) clutches failed
to develop as a result of damp or flooding; from the remaining 48 (27·6%) nests at least some young were
hatched.

"Nests are ravaged both by day and night. Diurnal egg-
eaters include olive baboon, marabou stork, black kite
and Nile monitor. Nocturnal predators include honey
badger, white tailed mongoose, serval and spotted hyena."

Troops of baboons, sometimes thirty-five or forty
strong, pay systematic visits to the grounds during

the incubation period. They quickly locate and excavate unattended nests, and may be seen running off with three or four eggs at a time. During these raids nests are ravaged in quick succession. Monitors are resident on the grounds and search persistently for eggs throughout the three-month incubation period. A single monitor has been seen to devour a dozen eggs in seventy-five minutes. These two species probably account for more eggs than are lost to all other predators together, but hyenas do much damage locally.

"When the hatchlings are not protected by the mother, they are destroyed wholesale, especially by birds—marabou, saddlebill stork, fish eagle, black kite, palmnut vulture, Goliath heron, great white egret and ground hornbill. Marabou inflict the greatest damage; they take possession of the grounds at hatching time, use their bills as probes to locate the buried eggs, and rapidly destroy entire broods."

Following this report by an international wild life authority, the Uganda Government ordered that tourist traffic on the river in the Murchison Falls park must not be allowed to disturb the nesting spots of the crocodiles nor drive the families from their basking areas. The numbers of baboons, monitors, storks and other predators are being reduced.

Operations against the poachers have been stepped up, and, despite a lack of funds, modernised wherever possible.

African rangers use light boats with powerful outboard motors. The poachers employ extreme and swift cunning—and harpoons with a detachable head attached to a wire cable and an oil-drum float so that later they can safely pick up the dead crocodiles which have been speared in the eye or at a fatal spot between the scales.

Extra ranger posts have been established, and in Murchison the park rangers have been equipped with two-way radio sets to replace the antiquated fire-and-smoke signalling between each other which, of course, also warned the poachers they had been spotted.

While strenuously combating human and natural predators, the authorities of the Republic of Uganda are making doubly sure the crocodile survives—for posterity *and* profit.

After independence, Uganda set up two crocodile research-stations—then unique in mid-Africa—near Kampala, the capital.

There is a bold notice at the entrance to one of these farms which reads: "Please do not feed, disturb or take away any of the animals." It is hard to believe that anyone might be tempted to interfere with the crocodile occupants of the deep concrete tanks within the compound. But when they were new-born and only the size of lizards several were stolen.

"I suppose children thought they would make good pets," said Fisheries Officer Bernard Ndugwa. "But they don't stay that way for long."

Mr. Ndugwa had helped to nurse the crocodiles since they were born in 1964—thirty-five hatched out of their shells the same day—to form the country's first crocodile farm. General protection outside the national parks might have led to an overbreeding detrimental to the lake and river fishing industries so the Government—its valuable export trade in skins having shrunk to a fraction of the £140,000 a year it once commanded—decided to raise crocodile domestically the way ranchers raise cattle.

In Africa, the phrase "crocodile-infested rivers" has become a starkly untrue cliché. Advertisements were published in Uganda's local newspapers offering

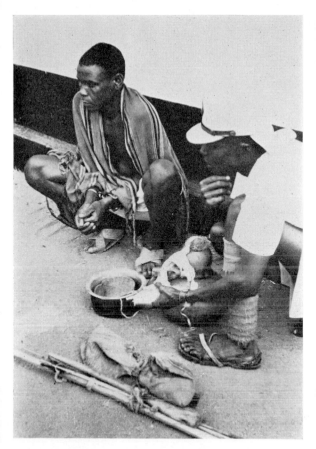

A captured rhino poacher in Tsavo National Park, Kenya.

Loomis Dean of Life *Magazine*

Samuel Ayodo, Kenya's former Minister of Tourism and Wildlife, inspecting ranger field force in the Tsavo National Park.

Marion Kaplan

A young civet cat in the Abuko Nature Reserve in the Gambia.

Orphanage ranger with baby cheetah rescued in Kenya's arid north by the army and brought to Nairobi for tending.

Francis X. Katete,
Director of
National Parks,
Uganda.
Marion Kaplan

Anti-poaching
patrol on Uganda's
Victoria Nile in
the Murchison Falls
National Park.
Marion Kaplan

5s. each for crocodile eggs or baby crocs, and local African fishermen soon began arriving at Kajansi experimental station with clutches of eggs and sacks of writhing young crocodiles. Each egg, with a thick white shell, was about the size of a fist.

At birth, the crocodiles were fed on insects and tadpoles, and they grow from six inches to a foot a year.

The crocodile is an expensive horror to rear. It takes 10 lbs. of protein to build one pound of croc— and he or she will devour about 1,000 pounds of food before it can be culled—at a length of $5\frac{1}{2}$ feet—for its 15 inches of belly skin worth £7 10s.

Feeding alone makes crocodile farming expensive. Those in Uganda gorged in their early days fresh frogs, fishpond production food at 1s. a pound and scraps of commercially bought lake fish at 5d. a pound.

The thriving charges are now snapping up condemned meat (the more rotten it is, the more they like it) from abattoirs, and buckets of a sardine-like fish called *haplochromis* from Lake Victoria which can be landed in quanitity for about 2d. a pound.

Each crocodile at Kajansi is identified by a numbered tag (no one cares for them enough to name them) and once a month they are measured and weighed by African guardians. Generally, the men scorn leather gauntlets when handling the young crocodiles which leap around wildly and thrash the green water in the tanks with their tails when disturbed or bare their formidable rows of teeth and give a loud hiss of anger when picked up to be examined.

Only a handful of each clutch survives in the wild, but on a farm the eggs are collected and tenderly nursed to a robust two or three feet when some can

E

be used to re-stock poached-out rivers and lakes while
the rest are reared for controlled culling. Under this
latter system, however, 5,000 crocodiles are needed to
supply 1,000 skins a year.

"I have never been bitten," said Christopher
Kaggwa, in his mid-twenties, wrestling bare-handed
with a three-foot long specimen and finally locking
its jaws with a wooden clamp. Kaggwa, who was at
the farm with its sixty original crocodiles, added:
"We have eight large pens here which have been built
in readiness for the day they grow too big for their
tanks."

Although females can lay as many as fifty eggs at
a time, they do not start to breed until they are late
teenagers so it will be a long wait before Kajansi's
crocs become an economic proposition.

On the other hand, Kenya has a 3,000 square-mile
"farm" on tap with 40,000 crocodiles—the 200-mile
long, weirdly jade Lake Rudolf surrounded by purple,
black and blood-red lava, the home of the El Molo,
one of the world's smallest and oldest native tribes,
who believe they are descended from the lake's giant
Nile perch. Some of the crocodiles in the lake are 16
feet long and a 20-year-old female produces about
thirty eggs a year; but the skins in general have flaws
and fetch only some £6 each. However, with such a
large population and the destruction of the nets of the
tribal fishermen, the Kenya Government is considering the regular cropping of the reptiles by African
sharp-shooters from motor-boats and on the gale-
swept shores to provide revenue for game conservation while protecting a native industry providing a
basic food supply to hundreds of families.

And, as the new African countries take more stringent measures to preserve all types of wild life, the day

of the tough, swashbuckling crocodile hunter of fact and lurid fiction is almost done.

For instance, tourism for scrub-poor Botswana, formerly Bechunanaland and the size of France, is a prime asset, and so the Republic is to preserve the crocodiles of the picturesque Okavango (65,000 square-mile), swampland as part of the country's showpieces of Nature. The reptiles, one tribe reveres them as its ancestors, breed in the backwaters of the swamps, criss-crossed by thousands of small channels and tranquil lagoons, hidden by high banks of papyrus.

And so Bob Wilmot, a teak-skinned 50-year-old whose domain for fifteen years has been the Okavango, has been told to wind up his business as a crocodile hunter. With Government permission to take up an area on the Tamalakane River on the eastern edge of the swamps, he has started to farm crocodiles for the skin trade.

One of the pioneer breed of whites in Africa, Bob hopes to have his first crop of crocodiles by the time he stops hunting. His killing licence total for 1970 is down from an original 3,000 to 500.

He is not all that sorry to be giving up a hazardous life. Crocodiles are said to be among the most difficult of African big game to hunt, having by far the best combination of smell, hearing and sight. Too much of Bob's life has consisted of midnight excursions into the black silence of the Okavango Swamps, spotlight in the left hand and powerful rifle in the right.

A crocodile's eyes are reflected, redly, above the water in the light of the electric lamp. A well-aimed bullet shatters its 2-inch square brain. It is then gaffed and put in tow behind the shallow draught boat which moves on in the darkness after its next victim.

Gazing down at the young crocodiles being reared in his penned-off areas of the Tamalakane River, Wilmot looks forward to the nights when the nocturnal perils are over and he will be able to sleep peacefully at nights again.

A similar crocodile refuge has been set up in Zambia which also protects the "much-maligned reptile that is more beneficial to man and Nature than most will admit."

Aside from putting commerce in skins on an organised and humane basis, the farms in each country will also supply near-to-maturity specimens to re-stock rivers and lakes.

Elephant in Casserole

How to save Africa's wild animals? One of the answers is—eat them!

African countries are compounding that seemingly stark contradiction by organising scientifically controlled game cropping programmes to ensure there is food for both the animals themselves and protein-starved humans.

Where game numbers—such as those of elephant in several parts of Africa—have become excessive and led to their destruction of the countryside, the principal means of guaranteeing the survival and multiplication of wild animals is by their strictly regulated killing for food and by-products such as ivory. The revenue obtained from these sources swells ever-badly-needed funds to help wild life in general to prosper.

An American-born ecologist, Thane Riney, who was one of the first experts to be concerned with game cropping and ranching in Africa, served canapes of warthog minced into a pâté and slices of corned wildebeeste as *hors d'oeuvre* to his guests at a dinner party at his flat in Rome.

The main dish was elephant stew. The meat had been simmered in red wine, and was served with a rich sauce of garlic, juniper berries and various spices.

After initial anxious moments, Riney was successful in his attempt to prove that African meat game is acceptable to even the most sophisticated palate.

The enthusiastic verdict on his fellow scientists on the elephant was: "Not just tasty, but delicious; like the very finest beef stew without its stringy texture."

The food eaten at that dinner party was from a wild-animal processing plant in Tanzania, one of the first African countries to adopt a policy of rational killing and utilisation of the carcasses.

Tanzania's overall programme, carried out under the supervision of game experts from the College of African Wildlife Management in the northern part of the country, aims at earning the impoverished nation £15,000 annually from 4,000 wild animals.

One of the college lecturers, Patrick Hemingway, presented a paper of nine foolscap pages to a conference in Nairobi in 1967 of 120 international game conservationists. It was entitled: "Some Economic Considerations in Game Cropping for Export", and the thesis particularly aroused interest among the representatives of African countries attending the symposium.

Hemingway made out a strong case for obtaining government funds through the commercial canning of Tanzania's surplus gazelle, buffalo, elephant and other game. He declared that his own experiments with home tinning of Thomson's gazelle had proved it to be "quite comparable to tinned grouse from a Scottish moor", adding: "One can well imagine a cold mayonnaise salad of 'Tommy' being a gourmet's treat".

As for elephant meat, Hemingway claimed that, provided it is put through a mincing machine and is well seasoned, it is "very palatable".

His thesis continued: "We have often served it in our homes to guests and noted their amazement when they were told, after eating it, that it was elephant meat. They always thought it was beef."

When it came to preparing a meat stew, elephant, declared Pat Hemingway, was even better than eland which can be domesticated and whose flesh often has the taste of first-grade beef. In the past, said the lecturer, elephant meat had had a bad name because hunters usually left the carcass of a shot beast until the next day when the tusks were cut out.

"Eighteen hours of stewing in its own juices in the tropical heat is not likely to improve the flavour of any sort of meat," he said.

Hemingway tied up the loose ends of his paper by listing the profitable side-lines derived from uncanned portions of wild animals—skins for rugs; teeth; bones, and even intestine skins for sausage casings. Africa, he maintained, could emulate the Chicago stockyards where it was a hoary joke that everything of the pig was used but the squeal. (Kenya has even taken that over. "Squeal" is the cable address of a big Government-controlled bacon factory near Nairobi.)

In Zambia, where President Kenneth Kaunda, an African church minister's son, takes a keen interest in wild life preservation, 500,000 pounds of game meat, mainly elephant, were processed and sold in a single year, in foodshops throughout the country. His Government has launched the most scientific campaign of the time on the African continent to crop thousands of elephant, hippo and buffalo in one of

the richest game areas north of the Zambezi, the
Luangwa Valley. This provides Zambia's victims of
malnutrition with food, free or very low priced where
the African families concerned are not destitute,
and the nation's coffers with dollars from the cow-
boys of Texas for boots and chaps of elephant
hide.

By now approximately 6,000 out of 23,000 elephant
will have been humanely destroyed in the valley.
They had been increasing at such a rate that
twenty-four species of edible trees had been eradi-
cated or gravely decimated, and scrub bushes and
non-protein grasses took over in large areas.

Twelve thousand buffalo and 5,000 hippo have
also been wreaking havoc in the valley where, from
1966, cropping operations have taken place each year
between May and December.

Hundreds of tons of game meat have been provided annually from an abattoir and refrigeration
plant on the Luangwa River. Nearby, African crafts-
men fashion handbags from elephant ears, and orna-
ments from scraps of ivory.

Other areas have been set aside since Luangwa
for culling following aerial counts of game, and the
Zambian Government hopes for an income of
£2,000,000 a year from them all eventually. Game
officials say reproduction rates increase as the herds
are reduced by cropping which is based on the same
principle as the periodic reduction of herds on cattle
ranches.

Baby elephant spared in the culling are exported
to zoos in Britain, America, West Germany and other
parts of Europe and the world.

Each day of every cropping season in Zambia,
hunters go out with special rifles that shoot drug darts

into the hides of elephant and other big animals. They sink to the ground anaesthetised. While still unconscious, their throats are cut.

The dead elephants are winched on to low-slung trailers, and hauled through the bush to the nearest track. Then, with the aid of tall, stout trees and special winching equipment, the animals are lifted aboard five-ton lorries and driven to the abattoirs. The carcasses are cut up, the meat boned and chilled in 50-pound blocks before being packed into 10-ton refrigerated trucks for the urban centres. Veterinary officials enforce exacting health rules.

Elephant, hippo and buffalo meat retails in the towns at about 2s. a pound, providing large and cheap Sunday dinners for African families of copper miners and other workers.

Death saves the elephants, too, in Uganda. Her Game Department estimates a 5,000,000 lb. production yearly of game meat (selling at about 1s. 6d. a pound) when all cropped animals are utilised, providing significant capital for extended wild animal preservation measures. And there are "jumboburgers" for hungry African schoolchildren among this republic of 9,000,000 people as thousands of elephant are shot every year to thin out huge herds.

Hippo steaks, also once cheap lunches at school, are scarce now that Uganda's main hippo cropping operations, during which 5,000 were shot—at nights when they come out of the water to graze—in the Queen Elizabeth National Park and 4,000 in Murchison Falls National Park, are virtually over after a period of several years. The average hippo can eat 1½ cwt. of lakeside or river bank grass in a night, but the numbers in the two parks have now been reduced by about 25% in each instance to figures the formerly

eroded habitat can support, given periodic levelling
out operations.

In some parts of Africa entire forests of thorn or
boabab trees have been uprooted by swollen animal
populations. Areas of the Zambezi Valley between
Rhodesia and Zambia (where there are at least 20,000
elephants) look, according to one conservationist, "as
though an atom bomb has exploded".

This happened in Kenya in 1960 when East Africa
was hit by one of the worst droughts in history. But
strange tricks are being played there.

Nature lovers in Britain and the world over,
appalled by photographs of thirsty, emaciated
elephant—"like walking rib cages", one report described them—in Tsavo National Park, scraped together cash sums for a "Water for Wild Animals"
Fund. Donations poured in, and soon water was pour-
ing out—from boreholes into circular concrete waterholes all over Tsavo. Yet no sooner were the boreholes
established than Kenya experienced one of its
heaviest-ever rainy seasons. Parched scrublands became large inland lakes.

After it all, the Tsavo wardens organised an
elephant count to assess the death toll. Parties of hunters sneaked up on herds and squirted their rears
with white paint while helicopters flew grids above
them and made the count.

The shock result showed that the operation to save
the elephants had been all too successful. There were
20,000 in Tsavo and surrounding land, apparently
too many for the terrain to support.

An American millionaire drew up a scheme for
putting an elephant canning factory outside the boundaries of Tsavo. But nothing came of this nor a foreign
scientist's plan for large-scale cropping within the

park, floating out the great carcasses on barrage balloons which guarded London from Hitler's air force during World War II.

The Ford Foundation was more practical. It awarded a grant of 200,000 U.S. dollars to finance research into how many elephants Tsavo, the largest game reserve in the world, could hold, and a team, under a British expert, conducted a trial shoot of 300 to examine the contents of their stomachs. Marksmen surrounded entire families, and on a signal shot down parents and young. None was allowed to escape to cause alarm and agitation among other groups.

The team, however, found that a few hundred dead elephant were not enough raw material on which to work, and in 1967 it applied for Kenya Government permission to kill off nearly 3,000. The answer was a resounding "No" from the African Cabinet Minister responsible for wild life who thought it cruel and wasteful to slaughter so many beasts to try to prove a theory that this was essential for the survival of the others in the damaged park.

Skittish Nature has proved his decision correct. The park's chief warden reported in 1969 that a fine cover of highly nutritious grass had grown up in parts where the tree habitat had been ravaged over many years. Deep-rooted trees are growing in place of torn-up, shallow-rooted trees. The return of the grass has restored the park's water table, and permanent springs are appearing all over. The elephants are eating and fattening steadily.

In parts of neighbouring Uganda, where the elephants also eat grass, there are as many as a dozen of the animals to the square mile; in Tsavo only two.

And research has now shown that the Tsavo elephant population reached its peak in 1946, and

has since been declining because the crowded pachy-
derms have been practising birth control.

Two decades ago, the Tsavo families were calving
in their twelfth year. Now they seldom calve until they
are between 18 and 20 years of age, and the gap between has generally been extended from about four
years to six or seven years. And puberty now goes on
longer.

Controlled killing of game may take place without
there being destruction of the habitat. It is undertaken in some instances merely to satisfy a demand
by the people for meat, by visitors willing to pay sub-
stantial fees for hunting (such as up to £300 for shooting a rhino, apart from £100 a day safari costs) or by
governments needing revenue from hides. And all
three requirements could be satisfied at once.

Herds of most species of animal will replace reasonable unusual losses (quite apart from those from
disease, age and the depredations of carnivores) by
an increased rate of reproduction. A fine balance
must be maintained, however. Grievous over-crop-
ping of crocodiles in Tanzania's Lake Bukwa led to a
shortage of tilapia (of the bream family) which is the
basis of that water's fishing industry. Without being
preyed upon regularly by crocodiles in accordance
with the normal rhythm of Nature, the catfish in the
lake ravaged the fry and eggs of the tilapia without
interference. Only a freak flood saved the tilapia
population from being wiped out.

The economic, and sometimes political, advantages
of organised game ranching as apart from culling in
the wild have not been lost on several African leaders.
Wild animal farming has been successfully under-

taken in southern Africa and, as a result, it is now fairly widely accepted that nearly all herbivorous animals in Africa are delicious to eat, provide good food for the many with empty stomachs among the people, are easier to keep than cows, oxen and other domestic beasts, and are likely to attract an expanding export market.

On the plains near Athi River, 30 miles from Nairobi, there has been a 75-acre paddock where the pasture grew so thick and lush that it looked untouched. Nevertheless, it supported a herd of 100 Thomson's gazelles. In an adjoining paddock of 150 acres, twenty cattle had left behind a miniature wilderness of dust, short grass and bare patches.

The two experimental areas have proved, among many other instances elsewhere, that game animals under proper ranching control can be more productive than cattle, and without ruining the pastures.

Zebras, for instance, remain plump and sleek even under severe drought conditions, and they are capable of producing large quantities of good meat even in dry areas where cattle would not be likely to survive.

Of all the continents, the prospects for large-scale game ranching are most promising in Africa, and the responsible Minister in Kenya alone has made it significantly plain his Government is convinced that "a high production of animal protein can be maintained from wild life on lands that might deteriorate under other forms of use". A leading Texas cattle baron, Robert J. Kleberg, Jnr., said after a personal investigation last year into the potentials in East Africa: "Game ranching can be made economical in Africa with predator-control programmes and the development of reliable watering places. Many African areas

I visited could support a higher volume of game population than domestic livestock."

There are now flourishing organisations in East Africa which are exporting game meat to America and Europe, and, naturally, part of their sales promotions are menus to popularise such dishes.

Mouth-watering scenes are conjured up: A roast, stuffed Thomson's gazelle lying on a bed of sweet potatoes and jungle spinach under an umbrella-like thorn tree in a tented safari camp at the foot of Mount Kilimanjaro. A dozen elephant, covered in red mud, browsing a few feet away from tourists enjoying a butter-basted guinea fowl, garnished with shallots and bacon rashers, on the terrace of Kilaguni Lodge in Tsavo. Haunches of venison served by scarlet-fezzed African waiters in a rest-house on Ghana's magnificent shoreline, in the dining room of the lodge at the lip of the world's greatest natural zoo, the volcanic Ngorongoro Crater in northern Tanzania, or on a balcony overlooking the Uganda Nile.

Saddle of giraffe has yet to appear on a menu, but impala, reedbuck, oribi and the kongoni (which looks like a woebegone Thurber moose) are particularly good eating, and elephant trunk in aspic is as delicious as the best boiled ox-tongue (although few Western people would share the West African's taste for a particular delicacy—stewed jungle rat.

In the bush, it is best to hang venison for one to three days. The joints—legs, haunch, loin or saddles —should be wrapped in aluminium cooking foil to prevent drying and as a protection against flies. The joint should be wiped over with a clean, dry cloth when ready for cooking. Pepper, salt, powdered clove, onion or garlic are rubbed in, and the joint is then covered with lard. It is again wrapped in cooking foil and roasted over a log fire in a covered tin containing a small amount of good stock.

An African in Botswana named Thomson who created a new bush dish has had it named after him —Steaks Thomson. His recipe: Prepare thick slices of venison, chop an onion finely and spread this on each slice. Then sprinkle a few drops of Worcester sauce on each steak, and beat it well on each side. Grill, or fry, over a wood fire with very little butter, and serve with a green salad.

Hunter gourmets in Africa relish smoked game-bird flesh, pickled in brandy (with celery, onion and garlic salts and cinnamon powder) twenty-four hours before eating.

The safari larder should be a large, square mosquito net suspended on the windward side of a tree.

There are many specialised ways of serving game livers, kidneys, brains and other delicacies, garnishing with such African commodities as carved coconut flesh, limes, banana leaves, cashew nuts, ruddy-skinned mangoes and slices of paw-paw. Natural juices, with or without brandy, form the basis of tasty sauces.

There are also scores of recipes for bush campers using only humble but conventional ingredients. These have been handed down by the African cooks of turn-of-the-century white hunters, trackers, porters and other tribal followers of the safari who learned to perform minor miracles under wild and hazardous conditions with corned beef, maize cobs, wild herbs and oatmeal biscuits.

Down at the coast the sea food dishes, too, are varied and exotic. But the fishes have their rights. . . .

Underwater Zoos

"It is recognised that the oceans and their teeming life are subject to the same dangers of human interference and destruction as the land; that the sea and the land are ecologically interdependent and indivisible; that population pressures will cause Man to turn increasingly to the sea, and especially to the underwater scene for recreation and spiritual refreshment, and that the preservation of unspoiled marine habitat is urgently needed for ethical and aesthetic reasons—for the replenishment of stocks of valuable food species and for the provisions of undisturbed areas for scientific research."

This verbose declaration was a main resolution of the first World Conference on National Parks held in Seattle in 1962, the year before Kenya became independent. The meeting called on the governments of all countries with marine frontiers to examine, "as a matter of urgency", the possibility of creating marine parks or reserves to defend underwater areas of special significance from all forms of human interference.

Years later, the Editor of *Africana*, the brightly produced official quarterly magazine of the East

Tanzania Information Services

Dr. Julius Nyerere, President of Tanzania, and his guest, Emperor Haile Selassie of Ethiopia, game viewing on the shores of Lake Manyara, Tanzania.

Marion Kaplan

Solomon ole Saibull, Conservator of Ngorongoro Crater—in the crater with wildebeeste in the background.

Kenya's President Jomo Kenyatta watching elephant at a waterhole from the terrace of Kilaguni Lodge in Tsavo National Park, Kenya.

African delegates to wild life conference at Kilaguni Lodge, Kenya.

A gorilla poses threateningly—Congo (Kinshasha).

Nairobi National Park rangers and ranger staff of the Wild Animal Orphanage.

Baby cheetah observes the world from the safety of a ranger's arms.

African Wild Life Society, wrote: "The time will come when the oceans must be managed, just as land resources are organised. To be effective, research must begin from the yardstick of what the seas were like as a habitat for marine life before the plunder began—before the blue whale was hunted almost to the point of extinction, before the yields of sea food fell so low that, commercially, they are not worth the exploitation. There must be, the scientists warn, places in the seas which are sanctuaries, just as the land's national parks forbid the taking of life of any kind. The seas, just as are other resources, are fragile."

In 1968 Kenya took the initiative among African nations in legislating to protect the spectacularly beautiful marine life that flourishes along its Indian Ocean shores, and made off-shore sanctuaries of its enchanted gardens of rare fish and underwater plants.

Marine national parks and reserves were established on the northern Kenya coast, stretching from Watamu in the south, with its South Sea islands atmosphere, upward to the great curve of Malindi Bay, playground of the package tourists from Britain and Europe.

The Malindi Marine Park stretches from high-water mark for about $1\frac{1}{2}$ nautical miles out to sea. The principal marine national reserve, which surrounds both the Malindi and Watamu parks, is 70 square nautical miles in area and includes a 100-foot wide strip of shoreline above the high-water mark.

The areas covered by the preservation laws had long been the hunting grounds of despoilers in goggles and flippers. They hacked off, or blew up with sticks of dynamite, sections of coral from the reefs,

F

gathered exotic, unique shells, and captured countless numbers of brightly-hued fish fry in plastic bags to ship them at handsome profits to dealers and private aquariums abroad. Thousands of the fish died every year on their journeys overland. Spear-fishermen, too, had been seriously and wastefully depleting the fish populations.

Overnight, the Kenya Government became guardian to hundreds of different species of fish—from the tiddlers of rainbow shoals to the deadly, torpedo-like barracuda.

In Kenya's national parks of the sea (and more are to be declared in due course) all marine life is given complete protection from poachers of all colours by African rangers in speedboats, and within the outer reserves only traditional methods of fishing are allowed. Spears, poisons and explosives are banned under stiff penalties.

"The marine national parks are to give protection from human interference with the underwater flora and fauna in the same way as protection has been given, in our many other national parks, to the terrestrial fauna and flora," declared a Government statement at the time the first underwater zoos became law. "In safeguarding this wonderland of marine life and its entire habitat for posterity, we are also adding greatly to the tourist attractions of our country."

Conservationists have been agitating for many years for marine national parks to be set up around the world to give threatened species of fish the same protection as rare land animals, but very few such parks have yet been established.

First of the world's tropical marine sanctuaries was the Fort Jefferson National Monument in the Dry Tortugas. Then the Bahamas National Trust set

up the Exuma Cays Land-and-Sea Park on the principle of the indivisibility of the earth and the ocean.
Other marine preserves followed, in Tobago, Florida,
Puerto Rico, the American Virgin Islands and along
Australia's Great Barrier Reef. But, until recent years,
only the authorities of the Barrier Reef's Green Island
could claim that *all* life was protected there.

Even in sympathetic Kenya it was not all plain
sailing before the new measures for marine parks and
reserves were enacted.

There was a legal snag at the start in that the laws
of the country contained no proper authority for
the ownership and control of land underneath the
waves, and it was impossible at first to gazette a
national park to include part of the ocean and the
sea-bed.

The department of the Attorney-General of the
Kenya Government, led by an eminent African legal
figure, urgently drafted legislation to make the formation of marine parks legal and their boundaries
enforceable.

It was introduced in Parliament in Nairobi early
in 1968. The Bill was put back several times in favour
of more pressing business, but it was eventually
passed without dissent and sketch plans of the oceanic
havens, "delineated, edged purple", were sealed and
deposited in the Survey Records Office. The measure
became law in mid-1968. The director of Kenya's
national parks proclaimed: "The protection of wild
life and its habitat is just as important in the sea as
on land, and Kenya's waters offer as fine an array of
tropical fish as any place in the world."

An editorial in *Africana* exulted: "Instant safety
for fish of a myriad hues, for coral castles which have

grown over long centuries and which were being
ruthlessly destroyed by carefree visitors.

"Fish-watchers had warned that an export trade
of the delightful reef fish was denuding the area and
they had urged strict measures. But full protection
was hard to provide it seemed.

"Malindi's warm seas and the long, rolling surf
would not keep still, refused to be frozen on legal
phrases and remained unconcerned about the legal
draughtsman's difficulties in precise definition of what
was sea and what was beach at every time of the day
and night.

"Yet now, edged in purple, the reef and its teeming
life can relax. What's more, lucky humans—letting
the African sun spill health and leisure over their
bodies can relax too, in the knowledge that Man
is being protected from some of his own destructive
follies."

In Kenya's coral parks of varying shades of red,
yellow and green live many different kinds of dazzling
fish, and an array of shellfish add even more colour
to the sub-aquatic panorama. There are the tritons,
the conch of Father Neptune (also called either scorpion or winged shells), the emerald and brown turbo
shells and limpets, oysters, whelks and mussels. But
the large tiger-cowrie and the cryare species which
were once plentiful—at one time they were used by
tribesmen as bride-money—have been collected for
tourist souvenirs in such quantities that today they
are scarce.

There are hosts of solemn angel fish, the gaudy
butterfly fish and droll clown fishes darting in and
out of thickets of russet and green seaweed. On the
sandy bed are turquoise and scarlet starfish, and
under the rocky ledges lurk the spiked brown and

white scorpion fishes which, as their name implies, sting dangerously. The anemone fish, which seizes its prey in feelers, is also on the lagoon bottom in profusion, alongside the *bêche-de-mer* sea slug, that prized Chinese delicacy, and a wide and picturesque range of crabs and sea urchins.

In deeper waters of the marine preserves there are shadowy remains of sponges and staghorn coral that provide the feeding grounds of the iridescent parrot fish which derives its name from its colouring and having a bony beak. Their companions are surgeon fishes and the silvery koli-koli.

Sharks and sting-rays provide the menace in the scene which is presided over by fantastic cave-dwellers—1,000-pound members of the cod family that have all the sneering appearance and Olympian manner of Colonial Blimps. The sergeant-major fishes—yellow backed and with black stripes—are but specks beside them.

Here again is the jungle with all its beauty and savagery, and the supreme law of the survival of the fittest....

In 1968, too, the trustees of Tanzania's national parks ordered a survey of the coast with a view to creating marine reserves similar to those of Kenya. Tanzania's coral reefs are acknowledged to be among the finest on Africa's eastern coast, but some have been ravaged by shell and coral collecting, dynamiting by fishermen, over-fishing and trampling by net fishermen, silting caused by upland deforestation and other factors.

Shellfish off the coast have dwindled alarmingly as a result of excessive collection for the tourist trade, and the giant sea bass has become endangered following an increase in spear-fishing by visitors.

The green turtle, already decimated the world over by the capture of breeding females and the taking of her eggs, has been hunted excessively in the past in Tanzanian waters and the State is determined to save it from local extermination. To this end, a coral island which is the breeding ground of the green turtle has become a prohibited area.

Another threatened specimen off both Kenya and Tanzania is the dugong, or sea cow, which gave rise to the ancient mariners' tales of mermaids.

In years gone by the dugongs, which grow up to 10 feet in length, were numerous, leisurely browsing on seaweeds and marine grasses in tropical waters on either side of the Equator. They have, however, been so persecuted and hunted by native fishermen with harpoons for their oil and rich, tasty flesh that they are now scarce and shy.

The *Encyclopaedia Britannica* refers to the dugong as *sirenia*, after the mermaids who would have lured Odysseus to his doom. But, with its yellow tusks, watery eyes and ugly, bristly snout, anything less like the legendary maidens on a rock—apart from the dugong's crescent-shaped tail and shapely hind-quarters—would be difficult to imagine.

It is a warm-blooded mammal that is completely aquatic like whales or dolphins. Many zoologists consider that it may have a common ancestry with the elephant.

The females suckle their young by two teats on the chest. In all other mammals except elephants and primates, these "breasts" are in the pelvic area. Dugongs have only one off-spring at each birth after a gestation period of about eleven months, and both parents show great affection for their young.

African fishermen of the Kenyan and Tanzanian

shores say they have seen dugong pups riding either on their mother's back or being held in a parent's fore-flippers.

The dugongs are basically shallow-water creatures, seldom feeding on any sea foliage below 40 feet.

Its blubber has been highly prized in some parts for hundreds of years for medicinal purposes; and its teeth, finely ground, have long been used on Indian Ocean islands for abdominal complaints and treating food poisoning.

East African Arab legend places the dugong—a similar creature, the manatee, is found off the Atlantic coasts of Africa and America—in a class by itself (as neither human, animal nor spirit) and endows it with magic powers, largely benevolent to humans.

Two dugongs which were kept in the swimming pool of an hotel at Malindi during the making of a film twelve years ago became very trusting and affectionate. At the end of the shooting, they were most reluctant to return to the sea and give up their human friends.

Once described as "this poor, floundering bovine creature of the sea, a delightful delicacy and a disgusting disaster that has been one of Nature's longer-lasting jokes", the dugong has for some years been on Kenya's list of protected animals. Yet so imperilled has their existence become off the country's coast that breeding pairs are to be given maximum safety within the marine national parks. The Kenya authorities have obtained information from other parts of the globe regarding the dugong's numbers, distribution, habits, and types of habitat to assist them in their campaign to save the "mermaids".

Happily, there are more dugongs—but certainly no gambolling colonies as of old—to be found off Tanzania. It is suggested that there they might be bred under State control in sea reserves for conservation, scientific studies, and eventually, perhaps, as a new delicacy for visiting gourmets.

We may soon be ordering "mermaid steaks"— medium rare?—in seafood restaurants.

"Let Us Not Regret"

The Tanzania Government's sun-bleached poster nailed to a fever tree shows an African father pointing to a herd of giraffe and telling his young sons in Swahili that wild animals will help build them homes, hospitals and schools.

This great land, where milk and honey are scarce, has earned global renown for its fine record in the protection and propagation of fauna.

Nearly 12,000 of Tanzania's 365,000 square miles have been given over to national parks (the figure does not include game reserves and conservation areas), and a record number of thousands of rhino are under her protection.

Tanziaia produces diamonds but, alongside these on Treasury balance sheets, wild animals are gratefully listed as part of the nation's wealth.

"Tanzania is not short of land—only a small proportion of its cultivable surface is at present being put to use," states the Director of National Parks in a report for 1969. "The parks, by and large, consist of land which is of little use for human habitation. This is the reason why it has been possible to make them into national parks with minimal disturbance to existing rights. From a national point of view, the best use for the land in these areas is that of a national park.

"If the history of other countries has anything to teach us, future generations will criticise us for having secured not too much, but too little."

Since 1961, Tanzania has received more than £1,500,000 from Britain, Germany, America and other countries in contributions to her game conservation work.

The Director goes on:

> "This support, which is far greater than that given to any other system of parks in Africa, has made it possible to achieve very rapid progress in development and in research without cost to the Tanzanian taxpayer. . . .
>
> "The national parks of Tanzania already constitute the finest wild life system in the world, and are constantly improving as more and more development is put in.
>
> "The animals are getting less disturbed by the presence of Man. They spend longer in the open and are easier to see and photograph. It is now rare for a visitor to spend two days at Seronera (the tourist lodge in Serengeti) and not see leopard, cheetah and wild dog, as well as the ubiquitous lion.
>
> "The buffalo at Mikumi (National Park), during the wet season, pose stolidly for close-ups and the Lake Manyara (National Park) elephants fill the frame of even a box camera. . . . The universal fear of Man is rapidly being shed."

In the past few years, the number of visitors to Tanzania from abroad has increased by over 160%. At present the country is getting a total of well over 64,000 visitors through all her national parks in one year. But the Director hopes for a minimum of 50,000 through *each* park annually, and this aim should soon be realised.

The Tanzanian tourist industry is expanding at a rate of 15 per cent per annum, and luxury hotels and safari lodges are either being built or extended to meet the influx.

More than 50% of the senior staff of Tanzania National Parks are now Africans, and others are under training for such positions at the College of African Wildlife Management.

"The future seems bright," the Director concludes. "Tanzania is proud of her parks and can look forward to their playing their full part in the development of the tourist industry and, ultimately, of the country as a whole."

Under Tanzania's energetic game conservation schemes, both the country's present citizens and those still growing up—the education of youth in the succour and appreciation of animals has a priority rating at the behest of President Nyerere—are being introduced to the wonders of wild life, principally through organised visits to the parks and reserves and audio-visual aids.

The Information Officer of Tanzania National Parks, Mr. A. O. Odoro, has a Land-Rover fitted out as a complete mobile projection unit. With this, he has travelled extensively throughout the country and reached mud-hut village audiences totalling around 3,000,000 with conservation documentaries and talks.

About half-a-dozen such films are currently being used, and a new one shows the various uses of land. It was made entirely in Tanzania with a Swahili sound-track and the theme is that everything depends on the land in some form, minerals, crops, building and the like. The film opens with shots of dead,

eroded earth and then the camera pans across to open
land with herds of elephant. The simple message of
the film is that land set aside for national parks is
being used wisely and economically.

"There is no doubt as to the effectiveness of the
film unit," said the Public Relations Officer of T.N.P.
"Because it is able to give shows in even the most
remote areas where film shows are rare and the people
unsophisticated, it has reached audiences who would
otherwise never have had the benefit of the information supplied. Such audiences tend to fall into two
groups: those who know little or nothing about
national parks and those with misconceptions
based on hearsay. In either case the effect is
salutary.

"Obviously, to many the shows are nothing but a
night out, but even here they produce an atmosphere
of goodwill which forms a starting point for further
interest and discussion."

The formation of wild life protection clubs is encouraged all over Tanzania, and conservation talks
in Swahili and English are broadcast regularly over
the national radio network.

New coloured posters, with exhortations in Swahili,
have been given nation-wide distribution. Displayed
in post offices and classrooms, they appeal: "Take
pride in our parks." One shows an African game
ranger in uniform and states: "Help him to guard
our riches." It is designed to create confidence in, and
respect for, the rangers and to dispel any illusion that
they are just another kind of policeman.

Organised groups of schoolchildren and adults who
book through the National Parks Education Office
in Arusha are accommodated free of charge in attractive, architect-designed hostels for over thirty per-

sons in the Serengeti, Manyara, Ruaha and Mikumi national parks. Score cards of animals seen (the lions sprawled along the branches of trees in Manyara always evoke comments of wonder) are issued to the children free of charge.

The hostels are furnished with beds (or double bunks), foam mattresses, chairs and tables, and are equipped with simple cooking and eating utensils. Food and bedding must be brought by the visitors themselves.

Each hostel has a projection room equipped with a sound projector and a supply of film, and the dining room is capable of being converted into a miniature cinema at a moment's notice. Film shows and talks may be given in the evenings, but the amount of solid education, especially for schoolchildren, is kept to a minimum at each hostel. The attitude of the wild life education authorities is: A child who is enjoying himself or herself on an eye-opening holiday is more likely to retain vivid memories than by sitting too long watching films or a blackboard. The practical results of this perceptive outlook are piles of paintings and enthusiastic essays from the children on return to their home districts.

Guides for tours around the parks are provided free of charge, and visiting parties are conducted through the small gatehouse museums of the parks by a member of the staff who is able to explain and interpret the natural history exhibits.

Although the cost of transport to and from the park—and children sometimes come from 200 miles away, over rough country—must be met by the visiting party, a subsidy of between £7 10s. and £10 is paid after it has returned home.

The Tanzanian receives for nothing, or a few shil-

lings at the most, what it would cost a tourist £10 or
£15 a day.

Under the parks education project the average
total intake at the hostels is 10,000 or more a year,
as compared with only 2,900 in the year 1963–4.
The hostels are generally full in the dry season, and
there has never been a month, even in the period of
heavy rain, when one has been empty.

"It's sad to find how many kids who come to the
parks in school groups in lorries and buses have never
seen a wild creature of any size," said the P.R.O. in
Arusha. "They invariably yell 'simba' (lion) when
they spot an hyena."

After a recent visit to Serengeti (in which then 14-
year-old Bobby Kennedy, Jnr., a wild life enthusiast,
spent a week shortly after the assassination of his
father), Sophy, a young African pupil of the Bwiru
Girls' School at Mwanza on the Tanzanian shore of
Lake Victoria, wrote a prize-winning account of her
experiences there.

> "We saw so many different kinds of animals which I
> enjoyed looking at," she wrote. "I wish I were still gazing
> at them. Some of the animals were very homely and
> hideous, such as the warthog who never faced us because
> of his ugliness. Some were so very beautiful that I had
> to fix my eyes on them for a very long time."

The highlight of Sophy's day, crowded with
animals, was the discovery of a leopard in a tree.
This is how she described the incident:

> "At my first glance, I thought that I had seen a large
> cat in the tree. It looked exactly like my father's cat,
> with the exception that it was bigger and his skin was
> decorated. I can say that the leopard is the largest mem-
> ber of the cat tribe in Africa I ever saw. This animal

impressed me so much that I opened my eyes even wider
than usual so that I might see him more clearly. I think
that he has been known to many people because of his
beauty. Tourists come to Tanzania to have just a glance
of him.

"Our lorry went nearer the tree in which Mr. Leopard
stretched. From this I could conclude that he could climb
trees like monkeys. This was now my hour of observation.
As I discerned him for at least ten minutes, I guessed that
this leopard was a full-grown one because it was so big.
From the tip of his nose to the end of his tail, it measured
about 6 feet, and if I could weigh him, I think he would
have weighed about 150 pounds. His tail was not so big
and it was about one and a half feet long.

"He had bigger ears than those of the cat. At both
ends of his mouth grew long moustaches which gave him
a fierce look. Although these made him look so, his beautiful coat still drew my attention. The coat was covered
with irregular black spots. These were more and smaller
on the head, and bigger and fewer on the rest of the
body. I could surmise that these spots helped him a great
deal. Yes, they made him appear to be a fine animal—
yet they served as useful protection for him. His black
and white patches mixed so well with the light and
shadow among the tree in which he lived—that it was
difficult to be seen by his enemies. Even I could not have
seen him if our guide, who was expert at tracking, had
not seen him.

"As I kept my attention on this animal, I realised he
had more means of protection. What very sharp, strong
teeth and claws he had! They seemed as strong as steel,
and a hundred times sharper than a sharpened knife.
These, I know, he uses when fighting, and I must pity
those creatures who try to vex him because he can tear
them at once like a soaked paper.

"My grandfather, who was a hunter and an archer,
used to tell me that Mr. Leopard can draw his claws in
so as to keep them sharp—always, or flash them out

when he wants to attack anything. He is beautiful like a ripe apple, but rotten (treacherous) inside.

"I could not see his eyes properly because he was fast asleep; then during night time he could hunt his prey and bring it up in the tree. Oh! this must be a very energetic animal to drag an antelope into a tree!

"The leopard can see at night in the dark just as well as I can see during day time.

"He must have peculiar eyes. They are as sharp as a lighted torch at night, and it is said that when one with a lighted torch happens to meet a leopard at night he probably can be killed because Mr. Leopard would think that it was another leopard approaching him.

"He had feet as soft as wool, and these, I think, enable him to move silently so that his prey seldom know that he is near until he attacks them.

"Now that I had seen this wonderful animal, I must thank my Providence, my teachers and the people in charge of this beloved national park who gave me the chance of going there so that I might see the protected animals. I pray Serengeti will never die."

A 13-year-old boy, who was in another school party which toured one of the parks, afterward wrote proudly: "People come to Tanzania to see our wild game because there is little or none in their own countries. In other lands—America, for example—hunters in the past destroyed almost all the animals, and later on people bitterly regretted this. Let us not come to regret."

A young product of game conservation work in Tanzania is John Ole Monah, a Masai, who was a cadet in the field in Serengeti.

John, who represents a few of the present generation with the courage to switch careers while it is hard enough in Africa to get even one job, had always wanted "to do something merciful and constructive"

A young monkey in the Animal Orphanage, Nairobi.

Buffalo in the Orphanage.

Don Diment

The crocodile pool in Gambia's Abuko Nature Reserve.

Sylvester Ruhweza, Chief Game Warden, Uganda.

Marion Kaplan

Buffalo stare stolidly at the camera— Murchison Falls National Park.

Marion Kaplan

Two young cheetah in the Nairobi National Park.

since leaving school at Monduli in the north where his parents have settled to tend their cattle and grow crops.

Moving away from the tribal pattern ("Most of my boyhood friends who have stayed behind in the bush regard me as lost," he says), John studied at a medical training centre in Dar-es-Salaam for two years. The course qualified him for rural medical aid duties and he worked as an orderly in several hospitals and dispensaries in Tanzania before being posted to a dispensary in Serengeti National Park.

"My interest in wild animals began, and grew, there," he said. "And so I decided to change jobs."

In order to qualify for advanced studies at the College of African Wildlife Management, he was a trainee ranger for two years in Serengeti, taking part in all kinds of field operations.

"I have helped to catch many poachers," he says modestly.

John Monah, a warrior who never wants to handle a spear again, has just started the two-year diploma course at the College and will be given a post of authority in one of his country's national parks at the end of it.

Looking eagerly ahead, he feels "that will be the greatest day in my life".

G

SOS—Grasshoppers!

Of all its natural splendours, the wild life of East Africa is the most renowned. In the great parks and reserves, and in the wide open spaces outside, roam elephant, lion, rhino, leopard, cheetah, zebra, giraffe and a galaxy of other species.

But outside the protected areas and the controlled hunting blocks from which emerge so many sagas of adventure and spine-tingling confrontation, of rare pictures and record trophies, there is another animal story.

The African-managed Wild Animal Orphanage in the Republic of Kenya, an institution rare even in the outside world, lacks the drama of the hunter's taller tales.

The setting is not spectacular. The animals in general are surrounded by open-mesh wire fences and, with each enclosed area or paddock having plenty of foliage and, perhaps, a natural den of granite-like stone, the effect is of a modest Whipsnade for waifs.

Yet the Orphanage is far from being a zoo. Not a single animal in it was captured or bought just for show; and while for many small creatures, whose mothers have deserted them or been killed by other wild animals or poachers, the Orphanage is justly named, the quiet plot of ground also embodies a hospital-cum-clinic, a maternity wing and a home for old animals—and some young ones—who have been raised as pets and whose owners have left the country or are unable to care for them.

The idea which has arisen that baby wild animals are reared in the Orphanage until they are able to feed themselves in the bush is incorrect. Animals cannot survive in their natural environment without fear, and most hand-reared creatures which have grown up without having cause for fear have little or no chance of survival if released. So the majority of those who grow up in the Orphanage remain (even for lions, it would need more money and training time than the officials can afford to adopt the "Elsa" return-to-the-wild approach). And in a number of cases they have now produced youngsters of their own. In this way, much has been learned about their breeding habits, gestation periods and other interesting features that would be difficult, if not impossible, to observe in the field.

The original, cramped five-acre Orphanage, near Nairobi, was opened with just thirty-three inmates on September 9th, 1963, the year of independence. Its objects were somewhat officially worded by its creator, the late C. E. "Bobby" Cade:

To give sanctuary and care to any wild animals that might be deserted.
To provide people, especially Africans, with "an immediate and effective means of education in the conservation of wild life."
To take over any animals that can no longer be kept by their owners.

The Kenyatta Government gave £1,000 towards
the cost of establishing the Orphanage, and the other
£1,000 required was obtained through public donations. Africans in the towns and country, including
entire classes of schoolchildren, sent in hard-spared
pennies and sixpences.

The entrance fee then was 1s. for adults and 6d.
for children, but the adult entry charge has since had
to be raised to 2s. to help pay for the food for an
animal population which has risen to scores of species.

Among the first inhabitants of the Orphanage were
Robert, a two-year-old buffalo, a three-year-old
rhino, a six-month-old lion named Ugas (Somali for
"Chief"), two steenbok, and three cheetah cubs whose
mother had been killed by poachers.

Soon more animals arrived. Sebastian, a young
black-haired chimpanzee, was donated by a Kenya
resident. Sebastian brought with him a bad habit—he
is a heavy smoker who lights his own cigarettes. His
behaviour is not always of the best (he attacked a
ranger at one time), but he remains popular with
young visitors of all races.

As exceptions to the rule, twelve of thirteen buffalo
calves which came to the Orphanage in the early
days after being rescued during a severe drought were
turned loose as robust adults in the adjoining Nairobi
National Park. They formed a herd there and produced calves. But the thirteenth, a reluctant bull,
resolutely refused to leave the vicinity of the Orphanage and its offices.

And there were a number of ostrich chicks—found
alone in the bush—who were reared at the Orphanage to young adults. For weeks after their release
into the park, the birds fed around the Orphanage
and insisted on coming back to their pens at night.

It was once decided to return one young lion to the wild, and an attempt was made to have a pride adopt him. The other lions, including a number of cubs, rejected the newcomer, and it was seen that he was steadily losing condition, becoming thinner and weaker. It was decided that he should be brought back into the Orphanage. Considerable time was spent trying to trap him, but to no avail—the young lion found his own way back to the Orphanage and thankfully went back into his cage.

"A lion is essentially a lazy creature, wanting no more than to be left to sleep for seventeen hours a day," said an official of the East African Wild Life Society. "If food can be brought to him, he can see no reason at all for moving. This is not to say that small cages are acceptable as a means of keeping lion, but certainly there appears to be little desire for the much-wanted freedom. Enclosures carefully thought out for an animal's requirements (as at the Orphanage) can produce a contentment unknown in the wild."

By June, 1964, an average of 1,000 people—and African families were increasingly among them, although the shillings spent on the visits represented some sacrifice in food or comfort at home—were visiting the Orphanage at week-ends alone.

On December 16, the following year, the Orphanage had its first wild animal litter. A bat-eared fox vixen which had arrived with a broken leg was delivered of fourteen creamy, wool-ball cubs. An oribi became pregnant at about the same time, a rare event in captivity and the cause for a double celebration. And in that year the attendance figure was a record 153,000 including 28,000 African schoolchildren who in the past rarely got the chance to tour a game re-

serve or see even a fraction of the animals that roam
their country. The Orphanage then housed more than
120 large and small mammals of some 42 different
species, and the authorities were impatiently looking
ahead to larger premises.

During 1967, when the Orphanage had an average
of 153 animals of 48 species (the figures change from
week to week as other helpless youngsters or wounded
animals arrive). African rangers brought in a day-old
Thomson's gazelle, a trembling Bambi, which they
had saved from the jaws of a cheetah after it had fled
under a tourist's car in the Nairobi National Park.
Alive, well and unafraid, it is still there—in a large
grassy and wooded enclosure among other buck.

The year 1968 was momentous for the Orphanage.
It gained an extra 25 acres of ground (on the other
side of the Nairobi National Park's main gates,
making a total of 30 acres), and its first African officer-
in-charge was appointed.

When Samuel Ngethe, a handsome Kikuyu, was
born in a village of reed-thatched huts at Kiambu,
about 15 miles from Nairobi, 32 years ago, his humble
parents could have had no idea that one day the boy
would be a significant figure in the New Africa.

There were many mouths to be fed in poverty.
Samuel had four brothers and two sisters.

He had to tend the goats and the sweet potatoes in
the family *shamba*, and he was thirteen before his
father could afford to let him go to an elementary
school.

The family lived in the Voi district, a hundred
miles from the Kenya coast, during the Mau Mau
emergency.

"I used to see lots of game, particularly elephant,
and I became interested in wild animals", says Mr.

Ngethe. "I made up my mind that when I left school—which I did after ten years—I would somehow get work associated with the animals of Africa."

With thousands of young Africans in search of employment of any kind, it was not easy. But Samuel Ngethe kept knocking on the doors of the Kenya Parks Department and, eventually, he was given a two-in-one job, as a clerk and a driver.

During the course of his duties, he met and talked to African students from Tanzania's Wildlife Management College who had come to observe the movements and habits of the game in the Voi area. As a result, he longed to be more active and effective in his work with animals. Finally, he gained admittance to the College.

In 1965, he won his diploma.

He returned to Kenya to take up a post as an assistant warden in the Game Department, being concerned principally with anti-poaching operations and the control of animals, such as elephants and buffalo, raiding *shambas* in search of food. Later, Mr. Ngethe went back to the Parks Department and became an assistant warden in Nairobi National Park, directing junior staff and leading control patrols in the park itself.

In July, 1968, the able and gentle warden was singled out to take charge of the Orphanage. (He is now furthering his scientific studies for the work at Bristol Zoo).

Mr. Ngethe, a married man with two children ("I suppose I got the job because I was on the spot," he says) took me on a three-hour tour of the enlarged Orphanage in the Spring of 1969. He spoke softly, in almost shy self-effacement, of the complexities of administration which includes arranging a careful menu for the wide variety of animals whose glossy coats and overall condition reflect the care lavished on them. Apart from milk, the Orphanage bill for meat, fruit (one female ape consistently demands a fresh pineapple—as a pillow) and vegetables is hundreds of pounds a week. That excludes special needs like the time when two lilac-breasted rollers were brought in after colliding with a car and the Orphanage had to issue an urgent plea for eelworms and grasshoppers.

And the regular chores of running the Orphanage are manifold. For instance, director Ngethe said that the meat for Brutus, a 20-year-old black-maned lion, has to be cut up for his dinner. Brutus is so old he is toothless, but at the Orphanage he lives out his days in yawning peace while baboons, marabou storks and vultures from the tooth-and-claw world outside his cage wait around regularly to snatch any morsels. He came there because the authorities heard his owner was bored with him and—although he still has a mighty roar—planned to put him down.

Looking out of place in the African setting are two shaggy, brown bears. They were brought to the Orphanage five years ago by the K.S.P.C.A., confiscated, because of ill-treatment, from a Brazilian circus which was touring East Africa. The bears love stews of carrots and meat, with bread.

There are other "foreigners", including a spider monkey from South America, privately donated, and an European stork which flew in—by a German airline—after it had been hurt in an airport accident at Stuttgart. There is also an "American" leopard, born and raised in Ohio. He came to the Orphanage at the end of 1966 through the guilty conscience of an American woman seeking atonement for the shooting of another leopard on a hunting expedition in Kenya some years before.

Each animal in the Orphanage has its own story, generally starting with tragedy and ending happily. If a mate arrives, there is often a family life to come. And there are odd friendships. A tiny reedbuck and a baby bush pig were brought in on the same day and, sharing a straw-strewn stall, they became the best of companions.

As we passed his spacious cage, Sebastian the chimp emerged from his den, grimaced and took a flying leap through a rope-suspended lorry tyre.

"There's little we can do with a character like him," said Mr. Ngethe with an indulgent grin. "He already has a mate in the old section of the Orphanage, and we are getting him another from Uganda. Perhaps the pair of them will quieten him down a bit."

The director added that he and his staff got their greatest satisfaction in rearing infants from the bush, of seeing a hospital case—like a gazelle nearly decapitated by a wire snare—saved, and in breeding from the many species in their charge.

Captivity—even for the right reasons—does not suit all the animals. Although several litters of piebald wild dog have been born to a fierce, needle-toothed pair, the mother has chosen to devour her pups.

"Last time she ate only three of the six—perhaps they are settling down," said Mr. Ngethe as we gazed at the noisome family playing happily together. These strange animals are certainly not the best-loved inmates of the Orphanage, but are tended as closely by the staff as the favourites.

One of the show beasts, which at one time shared

a specially built kidney-shaped concrete pool with a couple of adolescent crocodiles, is a male pigmy hippo which was presented to the Government by President Tubman of Liberia to mark a State visit to Kenya in 1968. Shortly after its arrival, however, the animal became sick and listless, missing the warm, moist atmosphere of the West African coast. After being restored to health under veterinary care, it was given a permanent home in the Orphanage in a large pen provided by cash donations from the people of Kenya.

It has infra-red heating in its bamboo shelter at the side of the pool. But its reed-bedding has to be kept damp to create the illusion of humidity. The soulful-looking beast also needs plenty of fresh food; since it spends most of its time semi-submerged, its pool requires cleaning at least every other day. The water must also be at least 65 deg. F, a problem during Nairobi's cold spells. On the other hand, care has to be taken to provide this droll member of the species with plenty of shade to prevent sunburn.

Another oddity in the Orphanage was a tiny, snowy-furred monkey, an albino vervet found alone in a national park.

Others were the three cheetah cubs seized by African game scouts from *shifta* (bandits) in northern Kenya who were going to slaughter them and sell their skins; a spindly-legged wildebeeste foal, fed from a child's milk bottle, whose mother had been eaten by lions; a trio of side-stripe jackal orphans brought in by Mr. Ngethe from a storm-drain in a Nairobi suburb; Danny, the comic, wing-tusked warthog which responds noisily to his calling, and a plump zebra named *Jamhuri* (Swahili for "Republic").

"I received a telephone call from a schoolteacher in the highlands of Kiambu, my home district, saying

this zebra has been found wandering there," Mr.
Ngethe told me. "It was far from its normal plains
habitat, and must have been chased up there by a
lion. We put him in a lorry, and he came to the
Orphanage like a lamb. *Jamhuri*—we decided to
keep the name the schoolchildren gave him—is very
happy and contented in his paddock. He does not
even have to fear lions any more, for the ones around
are fellow inhabitants of the Orphanage, safe in their
own pens."

Lying on a bed of straw in another enclosure was
an African kite—they look like cold-eyed eagles—
with a broken wing. It had flown into a wire fence
while swooping down to seize its prey, a small snake.
The tribesman who walked over a mile to the
Orphanage with the stricken bird would in earlier
times have killed and cooked it without a thought of
mercy.

"We release sick or maimed wild birds as soon as
they are able to fly again and fend for themselves,"
said the director.

At the time of my visit, marauding leopards had
been active in peasant-populated parts of the vicinity
of Lake Naivasha near Nairobi, and during the previous year nine such dangerous animals had been
captured by Game Department scouts, transported to
various national parks in Kenya and released.

Mr. Ngethe showed me a pregnant, fully-grown
leopard from Naivasha which he had in a compara-
tively small cage, with thick iron bars, in a clearing
behind the clinic. As we approached, she bared her
teeth in a snarl and growled with thunderous menace.
It was pitiful to see such a magnificent specimen
crouching inside a maximum security cage, but he

emphasised that it would be only a matter of days
before she was set free in a remote game reserve.

Earlier that month, anxious local newsmen, stand-
ing well back, had watched a seven-year-old leopard,
also caught near a Naivasha village, leaving the
Orphanage for the Amboseli park. Reporting the
tense, half-hour operation ("carried out without a
hitch under the expert eyes of Mr. Ngethe"), the *East
African Standard* described the captive as 'fuming
with rage, but securely caged" when put aboard a
van for its 100-mile journey to liberty.

To the reporters, Mr. Ngethe claimed the most
difficult part of such an operation was that in which
he was not involved, freeing a leopard.

"That needs a great deal of courage, planning and
pluck," he said. "My experience with leopards has
taught me they can be very *kali* (savage) when they
are out of their element and when they are pro-
voked." Yet his benevolent assessment of one of
Africa's most cunning and efficient killers is: "When
they are not molested, they are not bad."

Strolling back to his office at the end of a visit
which had brought us face to face with such diverse
wards as a white-tailed mongoose, a blue duiker
(buck), a long-quilled porcupine and a spotted hyena
(there are rarely less than 150 animals at a time in the
Orphanage), we encountered an evil-tempered male
Uganda kob which swiftly lunged at Mr. Ngethe
through the wire fence with its sharp horns as he
approached to stroke its head.

"Poor chap, we are trying to get him a mate," he
murmured. It was obvious from his expression of
concern that he was hurt by any animal's rejection
of his tenderness.

In Africa's expanse of wilderness the pattern of

life and death goes on undisturbed, which is as it should be. Yet conscience demands human sympathy and protection for helpless animals. For the helpless newborn, hurt creatures saved from the bitter laws of Nature, from the poacher's diabolical snare and for the victims of ordinary people's indifference and thoughtlessness the Wild Animal Orphanage is a refuge.

There a dedicated Kenyan, once a herdboy, is proud to play a leading Samaritan role.

Exit Obongi

Not every rhino protected by Man ends its days in peace.

"Obongi", one of Africa's best known wild animals, had a double chance of survival—and lost.

Nine years ago, her mother died in the West Nile district of Uganda. The calf was rescued from poachers and reared from infancy by game rangers within the protective boundaries of Murchison Falls National Park. I saw her, tame and warm-hearted, at that time.

At the end of her bottle-feeding, Obongi, a lonely and affectionate white rhino named after the spot where she was born, was turned loose from her pen. For a while she lived near an airstrip in the park. But, with her excursions along the dusty runway, she soon became an aviation hazard.

She refused to leave, however, until her closest friend, an African baggage porter, moved house to a nearby ranger post.

"Obongi never lost her affection for rangers and visitors of all colours and nationalities," said a park official. "She became so attached to humans during

her years in the park that she seemed to think she
was one of them."

Once in the early days she playfully tossed a
tourist, but, duly admonished by her protectors, never
repeated the incident.

Though living in the bush, she returned regularly
to the ranger post, and retained her fascination for
the park's crimson fire engine and tourists' cars. A
notice which was put up near Obongi's haunts read:
"Visitors are warned that while this animal is not in
the least dangerous, her habit of rubbing against
vehicles is not in the interests of paintwork, wing
mirrors or number plates."

It was the friendly rhino's trust in human beings
that sealed her fate.

Early in 1969, a gang of rhino horn poachers
who crossed by dug-out canoe from her early child-
hood area of West Nile, brutally speared Obongi to
death. The killers—in her eyes trusted human beings
—had no difficulty in getting close to her for the deed.
Her moaning and terrified 19-month-old calf (which
later settled with a group of rhino in the park) ran
off to safety.

Ambushed by sickened and angry African game
rangers, members of the gang—who were all subsequently sentenced—abandoned Obongi's huge body
on a bank of the Nile without being able to slash off
the object of her death sentence, her long, curving
horn.

She was murdered, like vast numbers over the years
in Africa before her, because of a persistent illusion
among people in the Far East that powdered rhino
horn—taken like snuff or sprinkled on food—is a
powerful sexual stimulant and an elixir of youth. The
myth arose from the phallic symbolism of the horn,

and it has brought the giant, armour-plated African survivors of the Prehistoric Age to the brink of extinction.

Obongi's only rhino rival in popularity had been Gladys who lived in Kenya's Amboseli Reserve. Although she was every inch a rhino and had an amiable nature, Gladys was a freak in the animal kingdom. She had a horn nearly 6 feet long, believed to have been the longest ever known for her species, and zoologists and naturalists and just plain curious people came from all over the world to Amboseli to see her and slap her hide.

Gladys had a friend, another female rhino named Gertie, whose horn was a mere 54 inches long. Roaming together, they were the greatest tourist atrractions Amboseli had ever known.

There was consternation among the African staff one day when Gertie disappeared, apparently abandoning her bull calf they had named Pixie. The youngster was immediately taken over and cared for (it seemed almost by tacit arrangement) by Gladys who by then had lost a foot and a half—the tip broke off among the thorn bushes—of her magnificent horn. Two weeks later, Gertie lumbered proudly back to foster-mother Gladys. She was leading a newly-born female calf.

While Obongi's fame was still mounting 600 miles away, poachers claimed Gladys.

Four men speared her to death when patrols of game rangers in the reserve were bogged down following heavy rains which had turned the countryside of volcanic ash from Mount Kilimanjaro into a quagmire.

The semi-naked poachers hacked off her prize horn, and also cut off a flattened ear, a distinguishing

A leopard with its antelope prey in the fork of a tree.

Marion Kaplan

Nairobi's Orphanage sign.

Marion Kaplan

While in charge of Nairobi's Orphanage for Wild Animals, Mr. Samuel Ngethe feeds warm milk to an orphan wildebeeste calf.

Marion Kaplan

Hostel at Seronera, in Tanzania's Serengeti National Park, provides free accommodation for organised groups of African visitors, mainly schoolchildren.

Marion Kaplan

Tanzania's intensive wild life education campaign includes attractive posters.

Marion Kaplan

A line-up of giraffe in Kenya's Masai Mara Game Reserve.

Kenya Information Services

One of Kenya's Cabinet Ministers, Dr. Julius Kiano (with camera), at Treetops.

feature, to hide the identity of their well-known victim.

The cunning gesture did not save them from vengeance. Enraged Masai guardians of Amboseli quickly traced the culprits and brought them to judgement. Each was sentenced to three years in gaol.

Campaigns in recent years (coupled with exports now of crushed reindeer antlers from Alaska and stag horns from Russia to help satisfy the aphrodisiac markets from Bombay to Peking) have cut down the rhino horn trade to some degree. For all that, the indigenous wardens keeping Africa's big game alive remain gravely concerned over the threat to the sorely depleted rhino populations by illegal hunters—forming the first stage of supply to amorous ancients in the Orient. The rhino's numbers today total but a minor proportion of its original, "Dark Continent" strength.

Governments in East Africa hold periodic auctions of rhino horns (which, actually, consist of thick, matted hair fibre and hide) seized from native poachers, or taken from poached, officially culled or fatally sick or mortally wounded animals.

Being both myopic and a sound sleeper, the rhino can be fairly easily slaughtered by an experienced poacher.

Each horn ranges in weight, according to age and type (there are the black and the square-lipped "white" rhinos), from 3 to, say, 12 pounds. The buyers at these sales are nearly always Asians, openly in the aphrodisiac business, and the average price obtained is about £5 a pound.

It is the cruel, clandestine trade which has reduced the rhino's numbers to a few thousands, and these in the main are now given the maximum

H

possible protection by African game guards in
national parks and other sanctuaries.

On a drastically shrunken rhino-horn market, the
prices paid to Kenya coast Asian or Arabic middle-
men, the underground agents for rich, unlicensed im-
porters on the other side of the Indian Ocean, are
now as high as £10 or £15 a pound. The poacher is
generally given only about 10% of these sums, but to
him even £20 represents considerable wealth and a
good reward for all the risks of killing.

In a recent year the vulture-encircled carcasses of
135 poached rhino were found in Kenya alone by
game wardens, rangers and scouts. Yet it is believed that the number lost to poachers' spears was
nearly twice that grim figure. In one area of the
country, thirty dead rhino—only their horns missing
—were discovered within a period of only two
months!

A Kenya game warden, who has spent much of his
life hunting rhino poachers, said: "We have naval
gunboats on patrol, but the coast is heavily indented
with lonely creeks. This has always made the smuggling out of rhino horns and elephant tusks a fairly
easy matter.

"They are brought down to the coast, hidden in the
bush or under the mud floors of huts by the poachers
themselves or middle-men. Later, the horns and
ivory are collected by other persons in the ring—
and are taken out to sea at night—through the peri-
lous surf—by African fishermen paddling dug-out
canoes.

"The trophies are then quietly hauled aboard dhows
bound for Persia or other vessels going to the Far
East. By a series of devious routes they find their way,
as packets of grey powder, to their customers: and

at a mighty big profit to the swarthy syndicates organising the whole sorry affair."

There have been times when up to half-a-ton of rhino horn from poached creatures has been stacked in the Kenya Government's sentry-guarded ivory warehouse in Mombasa, a smuggling hotbed. Customs men there who opened the suitcase of an Indian passenger staggering up the gangway of a Hong Kong-bound liner found it contained a pair of sandals, a prayer mat and a dozen rhino horns.

Cut up, the horns make half-pound handles—at £15 each—for Arabian daggers, guaranteed to kill an enemy.

In a spectacular and intensive combined operation carried out by the Kenya Game Department and the police in July of 1968, game trophies worth £52,000 were recovered in Mombasa from unlawful traders. The campaign led to the seizure of 7,000 pounds of ivory; similar quantity of rhino horns, mainly from the white species; 3,000 pounds of hippo teeth (they are used to make the "ivory" souvenirs sold to gullible tourists) and ten leopard skins.

Where the possession of an illegal trophy concerns an elephant, rhino or leopard the penalty in the Republic of Kenya is a £1,000 fine or five years' imprisonment.

African police and their colleagues in the Game Department had spent three weeks, working day and night, on their round-up—which was one of the biggest of its kind ever mounted. They searched hundreds of crates and sacks in and around the port area used by international shipping, and made a series of raids on both the homes and office or shop premises of suspects.

The first evidence of this highly organised racket

involving poachers in mid-Africa, Arab master-
minds in Uganda, pawns on the Kenya coast, and
receivers in Aden, Djibouti and Dubai involved some
stolen crates recovered from two Asians in the old
Arabic quarter of Mombasa. On opening the crates,
the police found a number of rhino horns which the
local game warden identified as probably having belonged to white rhino in Uganda, the Congo-Kinshasa or the Sudan.

In the "Arabian Nights" dhow-port area of Mombasa the game warden and a police inspector then
searched a house and store yard and found eight
boxes marked "Produce of Uganda". They were con-
signed to Dubai aboard one of the blue-water dhows.
The owners protested volubly that the crates contained a sweetmeat substance called "jaggery", as
stated on the consignment note. The game warden
opened the crates with a jemmy, and discovered a valuable collection of ivory pieces. (Those from big tusks
still go to America for organ and piano keys; to Britain
for billiard balls. Medium tusks—between 20 and 40
pounds—are constantly in demand in India where
at the time of her marriage a woman must have
several ivory bangles which are smashed when she
dies or re-marries. Small tusks go to Hong Kong for
carvings. Chopsticks are made from the hollow
nerve.)

The early investigation in Mombasa led to the discovery of similar crates being sent from the Ugandan
capital of Kampala, where one of the principals behind the trade was an Arab posing as a legitimate
businessman. He was arrested by the Uganda Police
on the information received from Kenya, but escaped
to the Middle East while on bail during his trial.

Further detective work in Mombasa—still a well-

used outlet in widely spread ivory and rhino horn
smuggling operations despite the vigilance of the
various African authorities—set the Game Department men and the police on a long and torturous trail
leading to warehouses in the crowded modern harbour of Kilindini. At one warehouse, leased by a clearing and forwarding agent, they found forty-three
crates stencilled as containing either "jaggery" or
"pineapples". They were packed with illegal game
trophies.

At another berth, fourteen boxes containing
bloodied trophies were taken possession of by the
raiding parties.

In all, the investigations led to the recovery of
ninety-nine crates. And it was found that the same
operators a year before had sent ninety-one boxes to
the same destinations in Dubai, Djibouti and Aden.
The Uganda Customs documents were forged, and
all the crates falsely marked.

The trophies seized in this highly efficient operation amounted to 5,171 pieces (more than the Kenya
Game Department handles in several years) and represented 250 elephant, 700 rhino, 200 hippo, and the
ten leopards.

In Kenya at that time there were only six white
rhino. These had been brought in from outside the
country, and put in a game reserve.

All the recovered trophies have been auctioned,
with the exception of the rhino horns. The sale of
these may be spaced out over a number of years—
to help satisfy the market and keep others, like
Obongi's calf, alive.

Rhinos on wheels

"The game laws of Kenya are stringent and strictly enforced to preserve the game for future generations", warns a Government notice to visitors.

Kenya is a showplace of Africa's wild life strongholds, and the responsible authorities—with every reason for pride in conservation achievements—resolutely intend to keep it that way.

"Wild life is preserved not only for its economic role in attracting tourists, but also for its aesthetic value," says the responsible Cabinet Minister.

In 1963, President Kenyatta, then Prime Minister of Kenya, gave a pledge in Nairobi to the tenth meeting of the International Union for the Conservation of Nature and Natural Resources that his new nation would protect its game animals in their remarkably beautiful settings. Since then the country has maintained a dynamic policy of conservation and management, widening the Game Department into territorial divisions and over twenty stations and substations with more than three times the staff that was employed at the time of independence.

A large number of research projects have been organised on specific problems of wild life management, coupled with education programmes to teach children and adults alike the value of, and need for, protecting the game.

Thousands of African schoolchildren and their teachers each year pass through an education centre at the headquarters of Kenya National Parks in Nairobi to learn about their country's wild animals, and courses are also held for members of the public.

Under Kenya's Wild Animals Protection Act, fully protected animals include all those "obviously immature", pregnant females and mothers suckling young. Females of lion and giraffe are officially protected at all times as are, among others, both sexes of cheetah, the aardwolf, elephants which do not carry tusks weighing more than 25 pounds in aggregate, the golden cat, the hippopotamus, the red Colobus monkey, and the hyrax or rock rabbit.

Big game hunters may have to pay £200 or £300 to shoot a single large animal, and the profits from such licences help to finance the conservation of other animals. Sportsmen are told by the Kenya Game Department: "Stalk your quarry, get as close as possible, kill cleanly and DO NOT TAKE LONG SHOTS (long-range shooters are bad hunters and should stick to the rifle range). Fifty to sixty yards should be the maximum range for all dangerous game such as elephant, rhino, buffalo, lion and leopard: get closer if you can. One hundred yards is the reasonable maximum range for other game: only in exceptional cases shoot over the range. Wounded animals should, of course, be shot whenever a target is presented. Hunt in the early morning; remember that animals wounded near dusk will certainly be lost."

There is a legal obligation on all hunters to follow up and kill any animals they have wounded. All visitors to Kenya must be accompanied by a licensed professional hunter when hunting.

The Act defines "trophy" as "any horn, tooth, tusk, bone, claw, hoof, skin, hair, feather, egg or other durable part of any game animal, whether added to or changed by the work of man or not, which is in such form as to be recognisable as a durable part of a game animal" and declares, as in other African states, that the following may not be used in the hunting of game animals:

(1) Muzzle loaders. (2) Bows and arrows. (3) Spears. (4) Quick-firing guns. (5) Bombs, grenades and tracer bullets. (6) Rifles of ·22 calibre (except for shooting birds). (7) Traps, snares, pits, nets and set guns. (8) Dart firing weapons.

An African official of the Ministry of Tourism and Wildlife told me: "Several animals, because of their trophy value, will always be subject to some illegal hunting. In this category, the most significant in Kenya are leopard, rhino, lion and, to a lesser extent, the elephant (giant tusks are rarely seen these days) and the hippo. These are protected by a complicated system of licensing which ensures that only limited numbers can be taken legally every year. Illegal killing of these animals is subject to very severe prison penalties."

Although there are several species of wild animals which have been threatened with extinction in Kenya owing to a number of factors, active measures have been taken by the African authorities to ensure their survival.

For instance, there are very few five-horned Roths-

child giraffe, a sub-species, left in the country, and
these have been found in areas scheduled for ranch
development. The various specimens have been ex-
pertly rounded up, and translocated to various
sanctuaries.

Black rhino have also been captured—by drug-
darting from helicopters—in parts of Kenya, like the
coastal belt, where their existence has been gravely
threatened by fly-by-night hunters. The animals have
been transported by lorries to national parks and
released to safety.

The Roan antelope, the sitatunga, a striped and
speckled buck, and the Bongo, the most brilliantly
marked of all African antelopes, are among the other
rare species in Kenya which have come under the
protection of the Government.

The crocodile, too, gets a security blanket. In
Parliament in Nairobi recently an M.P. complained
that his constituents were being attacked and eaten
by crocodiles in monsoon-flooded districts. What was
going to be done about it?

"Nothing," replied a Government spokesman in
the House. "The crocodiles belong to a protected
species."

Kenya also takes care of the animals of the bush
which would otherwise be doomed to end their days
agonisingly in fairgrounds and home zoos or pet
shops around the world after being trapped wholesale.

Life magazine reported late in 1968: "The wild
animal trade is such a flourishing business that last
year the U.S. alone imported more than 28 million
live creatures—75,000 of them mammals. The most
wasteful aspect of this traffic is the mortality rate:
for every animal that survives the ordeal of capture

and shipping, countless others have died. If the collector's prey is a primate, he will pick the baby because he adapts more easily to captivity, first killing off nearby adults in order to get at the baby safely. High-speed attempts to net swift animals such as the giraffe, rhino and zebra can sometimes run them to death."

Catching, penning and shipping are all strictly controlled in Kenya and, following that Government's example, in a number of other African countries.

Capture permits for game animals are issued by the Chief Game Warden of Kenya only to *approved* trappers and then only against orders from *reputable scientific or educational institutions*. The Kenya Government has announced: "Kenya is to ban all exports of live animals except those to public zoos and recognised research bodies. People intending to set up their own private zoos will not be allowed to take animals out of Kenya."

Broadly, former British East Africa can be considered as one wild life ecological zone.

"Although there are local variations in ecological conditions and hence game management procedures, our problems are akin to those of our neighbours, particularly in Uganda and Tanzania," said Kenya's then Chief Game Warden, a short, keen-eyed African. "We therefore have a system of close consultations between the chief game warden and the directors of national parks of the three countries. While we may have had a better start than Uganda or Tanzania in some fields, they had advantages in other spheres. And we are all ready and glad to share our knowledge and experiences."

Kenya's main, African-managed game havens,

which also constitute the leading tourist attractions, are:

1. *Masai Amboseli Game Reserve* (1,259 square miles). The name is taken from a dry lake, on which mirages are frequently seen, below Mount Kilimanjaro. The reserve is famous for its rhino and elephant population, and is one of Africa's main haunts of cheetah.

2. *Nairobi National Park* (44 square miles). It begins only five miles from the Kenya capital, and within minutes of leaving his hotel in the heart of the city the visitor is surrounded by most of the animals—with the principal exception of elephant—he can expect to encounter during a prolonged holiday in East Africa. The park is remarkable for its heavy concentration of animals (3,800 at last count) within a relatively small area—large herds of plains game such as zebra, Thomson's gazelle, wildebeeste, impala, and kongoni, hippo and crocodile in the Athi river, waterbuck and ostriches, wild pigs and giraffes, jackals and rhino, leopards and buffalo. The park is not fenced except for a few miles along main roads—and near suburban homes—to save the game from heavy traffic, and a drive-in cinema screen sometimes provides a stark, white dropcloth to families of lions sprawled among the thorn bushes in the afternoon sunshine. Cheetahs, once dying out rapidly in Kenya, are now prospering in the park, and mothers hunting with cubs attract rings of visitors' cars and Land-Rovers. The cheetahs often spring on to the roofs of cars and sprawl there in the sun. The Kenya Government has reserved a wild life "rest area" of 150,000 acres adjacent to the park to preserve it from human claims of housing and crop growing.

During a free admission day in December, 1969, over 18,000 people toured the park.

3. *Lake Nakuru National Park*. This is undoubtedly Africa's greatest sanctuary of the flamingo. Millions in-

habit the lake, the surface of which around the shoreline often looks like vast gardens of pink roses. Three
hundred other species of birds are also protected within
the park which has been described by the American
ornithologist, Dr. Roger Tory Peterson, as "The World's
Greatest Bird Spectacle".

4. *The Masai Mara Game Reserve* (700 square miles).
It has an abundance of big game on rolling grassland,
and the tribespeople are forbidden to pasture their
cattle there. Elephant, lion, rhino, leopard, giraffe and
the shy little bat-eared fox may be encountered. Concen-
trations of plains game there move with the seasonal
variations in the grazing. Tourists staying at the attractive and well-appointed Keekorok Lodge in the reserve
may see lions kill a zebra a few hundred yards away, or
look up from the modern, tiled swimming pool into the
beady gaze of an inquisitive elephant.

5. *Samburu Game Reserve*. This is the home, in
northern Kenya, of the rare reticulated giraffe, marked
almost to a third dimensional degree, and the graceful,
long-necked gerenuk antelope. Elsa, the famous lioness
of *Born Free*, lived in this part of the country.

6. *Tsavo National Park*. Divided into East and West
sections, it is Kenya's principal stronghold for big game.
The elephant herds in and around the park, which lies
between Nairobi and Mombasa, are estimated to total
well over 20,000. Scientists say this represents the
last great population of wild and largely undisturbed
big land mammals left on earth. The park covers an
area of 8,034 square miles and is 150 miles from Nairobi
along the main road to Mombasa, on either side of which,
in the Tsavo area, tuskers feed peacefully as cars pass
within a few yards of them. Road signs warn travellers
of elephants crossing, and on the verandah of Tsavo's
Kilaguni Lodge one has lunch with elephant, covered in
red mud or dust, wandering by in family herds at the

visitor's feet and with Kilimanjaro ("The White Hill")
looming above. At Mudanda Rock elephants water in
herds of up to 700, and another spectacle of Tsavo is
provided by the clear pool of Mzima Springs where underwater ballets of hippo and crocodile can be watched from
a wooden observation platform among palms and tama-
rinds or at a window of plate-glass sunk below the surface
at the water's edge. Walt Disney's "African Lion" was
filed at Mzima. A luxury tented camp is one of the new
features of the park on the eastern side.

7. *Aberdare National Park* (228 square miles). It covers
part of the picturesque forest and moorlands of the Aberdare mountain range and is the preserve for, among other
novel species, the giant forest hog. The park encloses
the well-known "Treetops" where varieties of game are
watched from an hotel in the Cape chestnut trees at
the site where Elizabeth II became Queen of England.
The "Treetops" lookout, with a verandah, restaurant
and bedrooms, is supported on wooden stilts among the
branches and a large water-hole with salt-lick below is
floodlit with artificial moonlight. Animals which can be
seen every night include elephant, black rhino, buffalo,
baboons and monkeys, hunting dogs, the white-tailed
mongoose and wide-eyed bush-babies. There is a new
lodge in the park called, and shaped like, the Ark. But
the animals stay outside.

8. *Meru National Park* (600 square miles). Noted for
its lush tropical scenery and a sacred lake, the park,
211 miles from Nairobi, is a reserve for white rhino;
and appreciable numbers of lion, leopard, cheetah, elephant, rhino, buffalo and hippo are encountered in an
area which ranges in ecology from tropical riverine to
mountainous rain forest.

9. *Mount Kenya National Park*. All the land above
11,000 feet around the snow-capped, fairy castle mountain, abode of the gods of the Kikuyu tribe, has been

declared a game reserve. The forested foothills shelter a large concentration of wild animals. Zebroids, a cross between the Grevy zebra and horses, are used to take parties of tourists and their luggage up and down the mountain ridges of the snowline. It is claimed that while a mule can carry two man-loads, a zebroid can carry two mule-loads. On the lower mountain slopes there is Secret Valley, probably the only spot in the world where visitors can rely on leopards appearing regularly each night in the glare of spotlights to take venison bait lashed to the trees just below the verandah of a blind. The leopards sometimes appear with cubs. Lodge fees are refunded if leopard, elephant, buffalo or rhino do not appear.

With the advent of jumbo jets, hundreds of thousands of camera-toting middle-income British, American and European families hankering for a spell of red-fanged adventure in the wilds have discovered the earth's biggest, most exciting, holiday game-land— Kenya—is but a few hours away from home.

The way-out favourite followed by Tanzania and Uganda, Kenya has a steadily rising tourist graph and is clocking up record annual statistics with floods of baggily-garbed game hunters who on fotosafaris get most of the thrills (but none of the grisly trophies) of a millionaire's safari at a fraction of the cost.

It is both the package tour, shutter-bug tourists in zebra striped mini-buses and the luxury caravans of tycoons out to gun down the Big Five who are bolstering the economies of African nations which have significant game populations.

In 1967 a total of 127,667 tourists visited Kenya which received £15,700,000 in foreign exchange from tourism during that year.

There were 43,516 tourists from Britain; 24,168

from the U.S.; 11,400 from Germany; 6,029 from India; 4,955 from Italy; 3,990 from France; 3,729 from Sweden and 9,387 from other European countries. More than 10,000 Africans, excluding those within East Africa, also visited Kenya during the year.

The total was double that of 1962, and expansion of tourism continues at the rate of at least twenty per cent a year.

Early in 1969, it was officially reported that, with increased fees and numbers of visitors, the Nairobi National Park was more than paying its way, and the general aim was to make the game parks more self-sufficient as the expansion of tourist revenue continued. Each park needed its own development and management plan based as far as possible on scientific investigation.

"Successful fulfilment of this mission," declared the daily *East African Standard* published in Nairobi, "will guarantee Kenya's priceless natural legacy being handed down to posterity, undiminished in a world of materialistic encroachment."

At the same time, it was announced that visitors to Kenya's national parks in the year 1967-8 totalled 253,692.

And the country's 1970-4 Development Plan published early in 1970 envisages a £37,000,000 annual income by 1974 from tourism, making the trade Kenya's biggest and most prolific foreign exchange earner.

The estimate for 1975 : some 500,000 tourists bringing in £52,000,000.

Leopards' Tragedy

Animals struck down or trapped in poaching (which in its higher categories is financed and maintained by non-Africans) are generally wanted for their horns, skins or teeth; some are killed just for their meat, to be sold slyly in African markets and villages. Others are slain for both sources of profit.

National parks and reserves where game abound are, of course, the popular hunting grounds of poachers, whether acting alone or in bands.

Giraffe are stripped of their hides for tribal shields, and the long, silky hairs at the end of their tails make coveted ceremonial fly-whisks.

Elephant ears are used for handbags, and men and women's shoes. The feet become hideous stands for umbrellas and walking sticks. In a five-star hotel or two catering for American visitors in Africa they are used as the bases of bar tables.

And a stricken, doomed giraffe, lurching on three legs and a gory stump after tearing itself free from a steel snare, is possibly no more piteous than a baby elephant squealing in anguish beside its mother which died a lingering death on sharp stakes at the bottom of a deep pit.

The animals are not alone in peril. African game

One of the tree-roosting lions of East Africa.

Norman Myers

Under the floodlights of Kenya's popular lodge, Treetops, two rhinos throw strange shadows.

President Jomo Kenyatta (in striped suit) and Emperor Haile Selassie at Treetops, Kenya. The big male baboon which has climbed to the viewing platform is about to take a sugar-cube titbit from the Emperor.

A leopard fixes a cold green eye on observers. His tail is the great give-away—rangers, with their binoculars, can see it from a vast distance.

Perez Olindo, Director of National Parks, Kenya, at the controls of a Parks' light aircraft.

The £52,000 worth of poached ivory, rhino horns, leopard skins and other trophies recovered by African game officials and police in a single round-up in the port of Mombasa.

guards are murdered or wounded, almost every month in some part of the continent, clubbed, speared or shot by poachers they have flushed from their hide-outs. Any ranger who tries to interfere with motorised poachers is likely to be run down and left for dead.

The life of a game ranger is of little account to any poacher—and some are little more than teenagers—as he can generally bank on the body not being found before the vultures and hyenas have reduced it to a skeleton.

Poachers in all countries smoke *bhang* (hashish), which grows as a weed in Africa, to give them courage for tricky meetings with the larger animals and face-to-face encounters with their pursuers.

One hard-pressed fellow in Sierra Leone jumped into a lake and hid under the water lilies. The game rangers chasing the man just waited for him to come, choking, to the surface and then hauled him off to the police cells.

When caught, a poacher will, as a rule, refuse to reveal the identities of his Asian or European "spon-sors" for fear of reprisals by a ring against his family. Collective fines on poachers' home villages are being suggested as an active deterrent.

African poachers generally build in a clearing tem-porary shelters in the shape of little beehive huts with grass, reeds and saplings. Wire snares are thick in the trees around these sinister, secret encampments which are littered with clay or iron cook-pots, muskets, spears (to kill the animals found alive in the traps), and bows and poisoned arrows. A new tactic is to poison waterholes for mass slaughter.

Strips of zebra, impala, giraffe, buffalo and other game meat are strung out on poles to dry in the brassy sun. Animals' heads, legs, horns and skins are stacked

I

in grisly piles at one side of the camp. Carriers come in on foot or bicycles to take the smoked or dried meat back to their tribespeople after paying cash on the nail. The stench of violent death is everywhere, and above the camps wheel the winged scavengers of the bush, the vultures and kites.

The huts are set ablaze immediately they are discovered by rangers' teams. The leaping flames cheat the birds of their carrion. Snares and spears and all other poaching implements are confiscated, and later destroyed unless needed as evidence in the courts.

In a single day in one area of Tanzania, seventeen camps, some of them containing up to ten huts, were burnt down by African rangers who captured 75 tons of dried and fresh game meat.

Should a meat poacher using a wire snare not want his catch (being unable to eat or sell it), he cuts the noose if the animal, say a zebra or a buck, is not dead. He allows it to go, probably grievously wounded by near-decapitation, not out of any sense of pity but to draw off the circling vultures revealing his site of operations to game scouts scanning the countryside through binoculars.

Some gangs use packs of savage dogs to drive out and run down the prey.

One of the readily available poisons used by traditional poachers is obtained by boiling for long periods the bark of the *acocanthera* tree. The residue obtained is like hot pitch, and when fresh is extremely effective on the tip of an arrow or a spear-head. For instance, an elephant hit in the side has usually keeled over, dead, by the time the poacher reaches it to pull out his arrow which has been treated with this poison.

Those African poachers who are masters of their evil craft are not lacking in courage and, as reformed characters, make first-rate game rangers on the "set a thief to catch a thief" basis. They will shoot an elephant from as little as 50 feet away, particularly if they are wearing their charm-bangles of elephant hair snatched from an earlier victim. The wiry bracelets ensure its ghost will never return to hunt the wearer who is also protected from being trampled to death by its living cousins.

Both using poisoned arrows, the pygmies of the equatorial forests and the other venerable little people, the Bushmen of the south, hunt as families. The fleet-footed, hawk-eyed Bushmen poachers, travelling with pack donkeys, strike down giraffe and buck with arrows smeared with a highly toxic poison squeezed from the cocoons of grubs dug out of the sands of the Kalahari Desert. The giraffe are cut up and carried away on the donkeys.

But, fortunately, most of the Bushmen are never wasteful in their hunting, and kill only as much as they require for themselves and their families. Birds are trapped by girls and young women, to whom the meat of a large male antelope is taboo. Rodents and other mammals are trapped by young boys, but the work of hunting and trapping the larger animals is all done by adult males. Their barbed arrow-heads are to a design more than 10,000 years old, and the Bushman bow-strings are made from sinews taken from an eland.

This large antelope is only tackled by poachers in pairs. It is considered unlucky for an African to be seen by the dying animal, so the actual attacker will remain concealed while his companion finishes off the eland.

The most primitive form of animal trap used by poachers and hunters in Africa has no mechanism.

The unsuspecting animal just stumbles into a prepared and disguised pit across its trail. The more barbarous type of pitfall will contain stakes of sharpened bamboo poles.

The "falling log" trap is equally inhuman. It is usually placed at intervals round pastures, crop lands and plantations—in a fence or on paths leading to water. The wild animal, in attempting to squeeze through the opening, releases the heavy log and is pinned down. It may be days before it is dragged out and killed. Other crude hunters set up a long fence of thorn trees and bushes and drive zebra, gazelles and other plains game through the gaps in which spring traps of bent saplings and nooses have been set.

More up-to-date bush butchers have been using Land-Rovers and lorries and working as well organised teams. Highly mobile, they kill their prey from the vehicles with rifles, shotguns or even light machine-guns and sell the meat and trophies—all in the course of a day.

As I write, a Kenya Police patrol has just fought a pitched battle with an armed gang of thirteen poachers in the North Eastern Province—where camels are used to follow criminals in the semi-desert. After exchanges of fire, the men fled, leaving behind a number of game traps and a heap of animal skins.

The Albert National Park (2,200,000 acres) in the Congo-Kinshasa, to which tourists thronged before the strife which followed the country's independence in June, 1960, had been in 1948 the scene of a similar, but more melancholy, encounter between rangers and poachers. Ten miles inside the park, seven Congolese game guards, armed only with spears, confronted a gang of 25 poachers, including a number from Uganda. The African guards finally drove off

the raiders. One of the Park's staff was killed out-
right and another fatally wounded. Found lying
under a tree where he had been knifed, the dying
man gasped as his fellow rangers knelt beside him:
"Did they kill any of the animals?"

After the tide of anarchy had subsided, the
Congolese set up an Institute of National Parks to
replace the Belgian body that disappeared with independence. The old and complicated regulations for
game protection and hunting control are still applicable. But it may be some time before the Government seated in faraway Kinshasa (formerly Leo-
poldville) will be able to enforce them, as in the
colonial days, in the nation's main reserves, the great
national parks of Upemba, Albert (Africa's oldest,
created in 1925 by King Albert of the Belgians), and
Garamba.

After depredations during the revolution years by
regular and guerrilla troops, white and black, who
shot elephant and other big game in and out of the
reserves for food, trophies or sport, poaching by Congolese and alien tribesmen alike continues to be a big
problem for the over-worked and depleted native
staffs of the parks. Twenty-two African game guards
were murdered in one major clash with poachers.

The Albert Park was set up, north of Lake Kivu,
along the Ugandan border, primarily to protect the
majestic mountain gorillas of the volcanic zone. Their
numbers have now been pitifully reduced by war and
human intrusion on their highland habitat.

Another primate species threatened in the Congo-
Kinshasa is the dwarf chimpanzee which lives in the
Sankuru district of the Kasai Province, in the heart
of the former "Heart of Darkness". It is, if only
largely theoretically, a protected animal that is in

danger of disappearing altogether after years of a
large-scale killing by illegal hunters, in or out of
military uniform.

Hunted ruthlessly by poachers as elsewhere, for its
horn, the white rhino population in the Congo's
Garamba National Park (for whose safety it was
created near the Sudanese border) has dwindled from
1,200 in 1959 to about 100 today.

The rhino situation in adjacent Uganda, which
also has a frontier with southern Sudan, is even more
acute. Poachers' hideouts are uncovered during low-
flying helicopter sorties, and the camps are system-
atically destroyed by a motorised force of rangers
armed with rifles. This year in the north's Kidepo
National Park, where anti-poaching patrols are constantly maintained on the ground and in the air, two
Ugandan game rangers and their two porters were
attacked and murdered by a gang of Sudanese
bandits. The ambush took place several miles inside
the park.

Poachers in Uganda are encouraged by a big and
profitable market across her southern borders.
According to the authorities, trophies poached in
Uganda are smuggled across to Rwanda, formerly a
United Nations Trust Territory administered by the
Belgians, and exported under licence from there. The
dried meat of poached animals is railed out in gunny
sacks as "charcoal".

In Tanzania, rhino horns have been found hidden
in the petrol tanks of taxis, and under 200 eggs in a
crate.

Special units are being formed there to step up
the constant fight against mobile poachers (sixteen
zebra, all killed within a few hours of daylight, were
found in the back of one captured lorry), and African

women have been trained to play their part as scouts in the anti-poaching campaigns.

The biggest poaching problem in Tanzania is provided by Serengeti National Park, the boundaries of which were drawn in such a way by the European administrators that every dry season each year from 15,000 to 20,000 animals, chiefly wildebeeste and zebra, have to leave its protection for the shores of Lake Victoria. A broad, teeming ribbon many miles long, the animals provide on their great exodus an ample harvest for poachers—from a single individual using a muzzle-loader, which wounds more beasts than it kills, or a well-armed mob in a truck.

Eighteen thousand snares, made from steel wire or plaited wild sisal, were confiscated and destroyed between 1956 and 1968 in Serengeti which is the size of Northern Ireland and contains the largest concentration of game animals in the world. Over 2,700 snares were seized there in 1969.

In May of 1969 it was reported by Tanzania's Game Division that ten poachers had used poisoned arrows in a clash with game wardens after what was said to be "the biggest ever" slaughter of wild life in Serengeti. The poachers were spotted while they were hacking up the carcasses of forty-two buffalo they had killed. When the wardens tried to arrest the men, they were greeted by a shower of poisoned arrows. One of the gang of poachers was, with a horrible degree of poetic justice, gored to death by a buffalo as he tried to escape, and two of his companions were captured. One of the anti-poaching team, who had been led to the spot by circling vultures, described it as "an unbelievable scene of carnage".

A warden who narrowly escaped being struck by one of the poisoned arrows was the man who several

years before had taken me on a similar patrol in Serengeti when, as I have described earlier in this chapter, the poachers' camps of tiny huts were set ablaze
(with due care not to start disastrous bush fires as
poachers sometimes do in the course of their operations).

It is not generally known that there is no antidote
for human or animal to the tree, bush or plant poisons
used on the poachers' arrows and spear-heads. A
stricken elephant, for instance, collapses before your
eyes like a deflated rubber animal.

In impoverished little Malawi, where more than five
per cent of the total land area has been given up to a
total of half-a-dozen game reserves, less than seventy
tireless African game guards have virtually eliminated
poaching. A first offence merits six months in jail, and
animals now protected by law against indiscriminate
hunting include hippos (a gruesome enlarged photograph showing the foot of a hippopotamus almost
completely severed by a wire-hawser snare was used
on posters in a nation-wide campaign against
poachers), the cheetah, zebras, blue monkeys, and the
leopard, which is featured on Malawi's coat-of-arms.
Many species whose numbers had sunk dangerously
low have begun to prosper again as a result of the
protective measures.

Although there is, all round, a measure of official
sympathy for the old tribesman who only kills a small
wild animal because he is hungry (and in some parts
of Kenya amnesty has been granted to those who
surrender the skins and undertake to give up illegal
hunting), courts in a number of African countries
have been instructed of late to levy maximum sentences of imprisonment—five-year terms are provided
in some cases—on hard-line game poachers.

The lechwe antelope of the Kafue flood plain in Zambia is a handsome and timid animal which when frightened runs swiftly with its nose down like a hound on the scent. The male—there are "black" and "red" lechwe—has long tapering horns, and both males and females are good swimmers.

The lechwe's hair-trigger sense of alarm is understandable. During their years of occupation (when the country was Northern Rhodesia), the British allowed the tribesmen and their women and dogs to drive thousands of lechwe periodically into the floodwaters of the Kafue River and spear them to death for food and sport in blood orgies. In consequence, the lechwe herds of the Kafue were reduced by 200,000 within a quarter of a century to a dwindling total of less than 30,000.

Under the African régime, the senseless annual carnage was stopped. Three years ago, a Zambian Cabinet Minister, after warning that he would take drastic measures wherever the "red" variety was in danger, ordered a massive air and ground sweep against lechwe poachers. A large number of arrests resulted from this swift and bold action.

Hard as it is to believe now, the pygmy hippopotamus existed in large numbers in several parts of West Africa even before the advent of the slave trade. It has backed away before the demands on territory of civilisation to tranquil water courses winding through the dark forests of Sierra Leone, Liberia, the Ivory Coast and Ghana. Poachers have hunted it to a point of extinction on the Bia River in the latter country. Its flesh is regarded as a delicacy and its fat, like lion meat in other areas, is sold in pill-boxes for £1 or more as a *muti* (medicine) guaranteed to increase the customer's virility.

African game wardens and their assistants are often asked why arrested poachers are taken away to the courts and sentenced without their relatives being informed through the local chief. The complaint is that "it is a worry and a hardship to the families who think their husbands and fathers have been lost". The stock, stern, if somewhat illogical, reply to this is: "Any person who breaks the laws of the country must be taken before a competent court at the earliest opportunity. When the head of the family does not obey the laws of a country, he forfeits our sympathy. You yourselves do not like to sympathise with thieves."

As yet the arm of the law stretches out all too rarely, it seems, in Ethiopia and Somalia. Belated efforts, however, are being made to tighten up and increase the game regulations in those countries— where animals of a number of species have become rarities.

The Duke of Edinburgh, who spent a week in Ethiopia in 1969 as an international trustee of the World Wildlife Fund, urged his host, Emperor Haile Selassie, in his lion-guarded palace, to accelerate the country's scrappy game ordinances and anti-poaching measures.

Although tourist-conscious Ethiopia has been spending at least £100,000 a year of late on the protection of its wild animals, poachers and trophy smugglers continue to be active. A handful of dusky and dedicated game wardens struggle valiantly to control these men, and to keep alive such unique creatures as the Simien fox in the mountains, the Nyala antelope, the Walia ibex, and the long-necked, bat-eared dibitag, also known as Clarke's gazelle, of which there are said to be less than half the number

that existed in Ethiopia and Somalia sixty years ago
due to the expansion of human settlement and the
increased use of firearms.

Another rare animal which still lives in Ethiopia
is the wild ass, considerably bigger and stronger than
the domestic ass. During his tour, Prince Philip
located an unusually large herd of twenty amid the
brazen science fiction landscape of the Danakil
Desert in north-eastern Ethiopia. The wild ass is
reddish-sandy in colour, blending in with torrid
wastelands, and has a black mane. There are white
markings round the eyes and nose, and are also white
along the belly. Black bands below the knee are its
most distinguishing marks from a donkey. Only between 300 and 400 of the species are believed to be
still in existence, spread sparsely over Ethiopia,
Somalia, and the north-west Indian deserts.

Savagely attractive itself, Ethiopia has been
charged in some quarters with being the centre of
Africa's illegal trade in leopard skins under which
40,000 of the cats may be poached annually—with
operators' rings protected in high political places. In
America leopard skins could be obtained by mail
order. Allied to a sickening past history of mass dealings in the black and white skins of Colobus monkeys
for rugs and ceremonial dress, these allegations have
brought her into wide disrepute, especially when it
has been claimed that 90% of the leopard-skin coats
being worn around the world are made up from
poached animals. Six or seven skins are needed for
some full-length models.

Ethiopia is anxious to shed this image while leopard
families remain relatively common in some parts of
the country, such as one 3,000-square-mile forest. On
the other hand, Ethiopian peasant farmers living in

medieval fashion in at least one area are said to still regard leopards as their only crop, trapping them openly without realising they are doing anything wrong.

One estimate is that 5,000 leopard skins were smuggled out from Ethiopia last year, and others came in clandestinely from Somalia (where this animal has been "almost exterminated", while "bare" and therefore "impure" elephant and rhino are shunned by Moslems), Tanzania, certain West Africa countries, and Kenya (where Asian shopkeepers complain they have to import skins from India to meet the tourist demand).

The heads of all these countries and other African nations accordingly supported a resolution of the International Conference on Game Conservation and Wildlife Management in Monte Carlo in December, 1968, that condemned the "mass commercialisation of animal skins, particularly those of the leopard and cheetah" and called for a drastic curb on the manufacture of women's coats and fashion articles from feline skins.

"Too beautiful—that's the tragedy of the leopard," states the East African Wild Life Society. "Too sleek in that desirable skin. With London prices as high as £5,000 for a matched set of leopard skins from Somalia made into a coat, there is no lack of hunters— licensed or operating illegally—who will put to death the animal with the beautiful skin. Inevitably, they receive but the smallest reward for their work in the long chain which ends in Britain's capital city, world main centre for the skin trade.

"London dealers say that even today, after conservation organisations throughout the world have threatened social ostracism of important figures in the fashion business because they 'wear leopard', coats made from the skin of this animal rate higher than either the Russian sable or the best of mink."

A number of smartly dressed African women, the wives of diplomats, leaders in politics and commerce, or professional men, are following the example of Nairobi's American "Beauty without Cruelty" crusader and blonde, wild life conservationist, Michaela Denis, who will buy only man-made synthetics for her wardrobe.

"To me a fur coat is no better than a lampshade made of human skin," she says.

Her followers, whatever their colour, agree. These women can still "look gorgeous in leopard" as the fur trade exhorts, but their coats, wraps, hats and shoes are of rosette-patterned golden and black nylon, costing a fraction of the real things and difficult to distinguish from them.

Yet, despite such boycotts in Africa and abroad (an American furrier has appealed to women not to buy a leopard coat for twenty years) and the unrelenting efforts to outwit and punish the poachers, the harsh, indiscriminate killing of the big cats for a stubborn fashion remains a poignant issue which the true story of an incident but a short time ago in Nairobi game park serves to stress.

A 6-year-old boy saw lying in the grass his first cheetah, a furry, female cub.

"Look," he shouted to his parents, "there's a handbag."

Goodbye Masai

They have rubbed shoulders with film stars. Ernest Hemingway, the American author, applauded the handsome, teenage warriors leaping stiffly four or five feet in the air in a ritual dance of warrior-hood, their oily, plaited hair streaming out behind them.

They have been photographed countless times by tourists—the tribesmen smearing red ochre and mud over each other's tall, stately bodies, the women smirking shyly in deep necklets of rainbow beads, or families drinking clotted cattle blood, mixed with wild herbs and curdled milk, from a gourd.

Now the image of the haughty, marathon-loping Masai indigenous only to the undulating plains of Kenya and Tanzania—gripping long, steel-bladed spears with which to protect their herds of cattle (or formerly to prove their manhood in single-handed, tail-tugging combat with a lion: today they are prosecuted if they make the attempt)—is slowly fading.

It is being replaced—in Kenya by official persuasion and in Tanzania by presidential edict—with 1970 models of Africa's statuesque "redskins", no longer half-naked in a thin, ragged toga but proudly astride a tractor in khaki shorts, smartly Western-suited as a political or community leader, or in a bush-shirt, trousers and snake-boots as a game warden.

In both countries, which share more than a quarter of a million Masai, the men and their families are beng wooed by posters and propaganda campaigns from the nomadic life, which took heavy toll of the game, to wild life conservation and farming and veterinary courses, adult literacy centres, homecraft and modern cooking classes and general nation-building projects like the construction of roads, schools and clinics.

Governmental efforts have long been directed in increasing measure at getting Masai faction and families to settle down and not wander the country-side with hundreds of thousands of domestic beasts, creating dead lands and depriving the game of their habitats.

The Masai, who draw the blood for their staple diet from the pierced jugular veins—afterwards sealed with mud—of their cows, have in the past been the chief offenders in jeopardising East Africa's wild animals by over-grazing.

One of their dying rites is the *ewunoto* ceremony, wild and secret, which used to take place every seven years. Marking the creation of a new generation of "junior elders", the *ewunoto* represents the "cleansing" phase at the end of a series of ceremonies designed to ensure the young Masai will become a loyal and hard-working member of the tribe.

At one of the last performances in Kenya, thousands of the tribespeople gathered in a clearing in the bush and squatted in a huge circle as the youthful warriors stamped out their final dances as *morani* whose traditional killing of a lion, banned by the African authorities, is now no more than shadow-play. Then, behind a screen of tall bushes, tribal headmen tied cow-hide thongs round the middle fingers of the initiates, ghostly in white ash, their nude bodies decorated with elaborate designs. The thongs were the outward signs of their new, elevated status.

Finally, the new young leaders snaked down from a wind-swept escarpment, leaping and chanting in grotesque masks and head-dresses of black and white feathers as their crimson capes of thin calico billowed out behind them. Comely young brides-to-be joined in the roar of acclaim which greeted them.

Nothing is being done at government levels to revive the *ewunoto*, which is becoming a rarely-performed spectacle, mainly for tourists, as the Masai move with ever-lengthening strides into the twentieth century.

Shapashina Ole Oloitipitip became a leader of Kenya's Masai by virtue of having killed five lions. Nowadays he would think twice about swatting a fly, and it was through the polls that he became a Member of Parliament and later Assistant Minister for Commerce and Industry.

Although he still wore his cloth toga when among his wives and children in the bush, Mr. Oloitipitip was proudly attired in a well-cut dark-cloth business suit in Parliament and the streets of Nairobi. "The Masai are all out for progress," he says.

Spurred on by the Kenya Government, his people struggle valiantly in an economic race to catch up with the rest of the country.

Masailand in Kenya covers some 15,000 square miles divided into a number of districts. The African Government has sunk boreholes in all these parts

Marion Kaplan

In the Nairobi National Park: the Wildlife Education bus taking children on a tour of the park.

Marion Kaplan

A rhino in the Nairobi National Park watched by fascinated African schoolchildren.

Marion Kaplan

Christopher Manu of Ghana at the Wildlife Management College, Mweka, Tanzania.

Norman Myers

An old bull elephant, which has lost half of one tusk in a mating battle, at the foot of Mount Kilimanjaro, Tanzania.

A hungry leopard in Tanzania's Serengeti National Park stretches himself at dusk and surveys a herd of gazelles.

Students at the College of African Wildlife Management at Mweka, Tanzania.

Marion Kaplan

Masai Warrior.

to alleviate serious water problems which originally
turned the Masai into wanderers with thirsty cattle
that drove away the game from the natural waterholes and cropped their herbage to the roots.

The Kenya Masai—whether inter-bred or not with
the Kikuyu, or share-cropping with them—continue
to develop on an agricultural basis, creating in ever-
increasing numbers settled or semi-settled communities with maize, wheat or cattle farms. And where
there is a borehole the gipsy Masai become involved
with established social amenities like schools and
health centres.

An energetic Community Development Officer, a
Masai woman, in a white blouse and dark green skirt,
whose father, nevertheless, was a noted warrior who
slew men and big game alike, told me: "You have to
provide water before any other form of development
can take shape. Otherwise the Masai will start moving again.

"The percentage of settled—or even, shall we say,
less restless—Masai has not yet been officially calcu-
lated. But the significant thing—for my people and
the wild animals—is that we know it is rising steadily
all the time."

This is clearly evidenced by the fact that ranches
of a thousand acres or so—run by a group of inter-
related Masai (they are dyed in the wool "family
socialists") or a co-operative society—are to be found
more and more on the savannah lands of Kajiado,
Narok, Ngong and elsewhere.

Wheat growing in Kenya's Masailand is a com-
paratively new venture, but it is indicative of the
once shiftless tribe's acceptance and adoption of static
farming. Only a few miles from Ngong township near
Nairobi, a group of twenty pioneer Masai farmers

K

grew excellent wheat on a 70-acre farm, and elsewhere in the Ngong division forty members of a
Masai co-operative have been running a 300-acre
wheat farm. There are many other examples of such
settled enterprise.

Demarcation has to be effected to facilitate non-
pastoral development, and in the Ngong division
alone a total of 27,000 acres made up the original
allocation of land to individual Masai or group
owners. Said a senior Lands Department official:
"What is most striking is the fact that the Masai—
who until recently knew nothing of title deeds or land
boundaries—have so readily accepted the plan."

State and private loans have been offered for a
couple of years now to Masai would-be farmers and
ranchers to encourage even more nomads and their
families to put down their roots. Sums ranging from
£500 to £300 (fortunes in the eyes of peasant Africans) are regularly advanced to individuals for these
purposes, and applications continue to mount as others
prepare to shake the dust of ravaged soil off their
bare feet.

Although in the past they have been roundly
accused as the chief culprits among native tribes in
their indifference to the fate of the game, the Masai
are now playing prominent roles in the programmes
for animal conservation.

In Kenya, for instance, one of the first and most
energetic junior Ministers for Tourism and Wildlife
was a Masai, and his brother was put in charge of a
700-square-mile game animal haven in the heart of
Masai-land.

The post-independence warden of the famous
Amboseli Game Reserve on the Kenya side of Mount
Kilimanjaro was another Masai who was instrumen-

tal in saving the rhino and thousands of other animals
there from his fellow tribespeople who were apt to
drive their herds across the sanctuary and to start disastrous bush fires by carelessly failing to extinguish
the embers in their cooking trenches when they moved
on. Now the Masai are moving back to allow Amboseli to expand.

Masai ex-warriors are employed throughout Kenya
as game scouts and keen-eyed members of anti-
poaching patrols. They can spot a cheetah under a
tree a quarter of a mile away.

A number of game reserves in East Africa, such
as the Masai Amboseli, are run by local African
councils consisting of both snowy-headed elders and
eager young politicians.

In Tanzania a sum of £500,000 has been earmarked for animal husbandry among the country's
100,000 Masai, found predominantly in the northern
part of the nation around Arusha, and large sums
have already been spent by the Government to provide water, that vital stabilising factor, for the Nilo-
Hamitic cattlemen.

Determined to create "one nation" and to eradicate
"diversive tribalism" throughout the land, President
Nyerere last year ordered the Masai to adopt
trousers, coats and other forms of "civilised dress" (he
even decreed that the imprint of a scantily clad Masai
warrior be removed from Tanzania's 100s. notes) in
line with abandoning their ageless wanderings. His
50-year-old African Regional Commissioner in
Arusha threatened any bare-buttock Masai with
public washings, locked up in the police cells any
men or women who did not cover up with a tawdry
ex-British Army greatcoat, or a sack-like, ankle-
length dress and declared: "The Masai are not

curios or fancy masks to attract the attention of
foreigners." The Commissioner, a member of a tribe
once servile to the warlike Masai, led a symbolic
procession of black citizens through Arusha (the
administrative town exactly half-way between Cape-
town and Cairo), to dump $1\frac{1}{2}$ tons of red ochre powder
worth £250 into a nearby river.

He sternly instructed the Masai to:

1. Refuse to allow tourists to take "your naked pictures".
   However, blood-drinking could go on as a "nutritional
   main diet".

2. Abandon lion-killing initiation ceremonies. ("This,"
   he said, "was, perhaps, a good tradition when lions
   were more plentiful and threatened villages because it
   taught the aspirant young members of the Masai regi-
   ments to be particularly courageous: but it was also
   used to train them to steal cattle, causing wars with
   other tribes.") Instead of initiation rites for battles,
   young Masai are now being drafted in increasing
   numbers into Tanzania's quasi-military National Service organisations where instead of a strip of loin-cloth
   or *shuka* they wear floppy jungle hats, infantry boots
   and a type of British battle-dress in drab-green.

3. Give up cattle rustling. (The Masai are among Africa's
   most skilled stock thieves.)

Subsequently, there were no Masai in tribal regalia
among the throng of tens of thousands who turned
out, dancing and singing, when three East African
heads of state visited Arusha shortly after the decree.
The heavily-perspiring Masai women wore gaudy
brassières under shoulder-to-toe gowns, and among
the crowd were cowboy outfits, leopard-print head-
scarves, tattered shorts, double-breasted, second-hand
suits from the open-air market, and snap-brim hats.

One proud Masai of the new social order sported a green tweed jacket, a sky-blue plastic trilby, a brown blanket "skirt" and a yellow film canister in the hole in the lobe of his ear where his heavy, beaded earrings should have been. There was never a gaily painted hide shield, a hunting knife or a shred of red cloth to be seen.

Thundered the daily newspaper of Nyerere's ruling party: "Our former colonial masters wanted to maintain Masailand as a human zoo for themselves and their children", a bitter tilt at the fact that many colonialists and their wives did develop a Masai fetish—a Blimpish affection for the noble savage which was more an affectation—during their years of trusteeship in what was then Tangankiya.

The African Commissioner in Arusha later proudly reported: "The campaign to get the Masai to change their habits has been very successful, and the Masai themselves are very grateful for being civilised."

Today more than a handful of Masai—markedly intelligent as befits an élite—are pioneering the roads to emancipation and success in Tanzania.

The first Masai to hold a ministerial post in the Nyerere régime was Mr. Edward M. Sokoine. He has horseshoe tribal scars on each cheek but adopted the Chinese-type, pyjama suit style of dress favoured by the President who blessed the appointment of Sokoine, moon-faced, mild-mannered and 6 feet tall, as Junior Minister (for Communications and Works) with a flourish of his blackwood cudgel, the Masai peacemaker's stick, which the Tanzanian leader invariably carries around with him.

Mr. Sokoine, in his early thirties, speaks English softly and well. From the beginning, he has been a whole-hearted supporter of Nyerere's reform programme in the 23,000 square miles of Tanzania Masailand. He projects the image of a modern Masai intellectual and claims never to have daubed himself with red ochre.

"Women and the younger men were the chief culprits," he says. Sokoine, who before joining the Government was engaged in welfare work among his people, did much to persuade them to accept compulsory schooling for their children. "Education is the only way to throw off the past completely and wean all the Masai away from the old tribal dress and customs. Strangely enough, it is the older Masai who have been giving the lead in forswearing the ancient habits."

The police officers in charge of Moshi District below Kilimanjaro—the chief enemy of all game poachers in the area—have long been Masai.

Tall (as becomes a true Masai), a woolly-haired Chief Edward Mbarnoti, middle-aged "Great Speaker of the Masai", did not have to express his views on President Nyerere's drive to modernise and settle the nomads. Vigorously signifying his support, Chief Mbarnoti pointed to his grey trousers, white shirt and blue, knitted pullover as he moved among the picture-postcard elders and *moran* of his people on the emerald pastures around Monduli, which has become the centre—mission stations surrounded by thatched, mud-walled huts—of the rural Masai in Tanzania.

"We want no more giant dust-bowls, but more and more permanent villages like Monduli," said the chief who has played a prominent and eager role in teaching the Masai the advantages of "planting the spear in the ground" and taking up mechanised wheat and maize farming.

Masai schoolchildren at Monduli have, significantly, established a model farm with experimental vegetable plots and poultry runs. They have planted their own forests—to provide firewood (East Africa has virtually no coal) when they are adults.

The Masai tribesmen of old—towering against the skyline as a blood-red African sunset matched and set aglow his pigment—was a significant figure in the sorely needed revenue from Tanzania's tourist industry. But with his passing into modernity—as the haze begins to settle, the cattle are driven into stockades, and the spears no longer flash—the wild animals, and the profits to a virile African socialist state, can only multiply.

The Man who talks to Lions

He is a full-blooded Masai warrior, the holder of a Bachelor of Arts degree, and he can trade light conversation with lions. Stocky and black-bearded, he is also "king" over man and beast in a "Garden of Eden" domain of this Lunar Age. And he looks none of these parts.

Solomon ole Saibull, 35, has the gaze and features of a mystic, but is as robust as a yeoman. Instead of swathing himself in the flame-coloured cloths of his famous tribe or donning some gilt-braided uniform as a symbol of his high authority, Mr. Saibull, a bachelor, is usually to be found in brogues or sandals, a baggy pair of fawn trousers, a dark green shirt, and a hairy, faded pullover which had once been of full mustard glory.

At an age when children of the West are in nursery school, he was rounding up cows, steers and calves, barefoot and as naked as a cherub except for a few wisps of calico.

He is now Conservator—the first African to hold

the post—of Tanzania's Masai-occupied Ngorongoro
Conservation Area, the heart of which, at 7,500 feet
above sea level, is the world's second largest crater.
There, in a setting of Olympian grandeur dotted with
wild flowers from orchids to lupins, the game herds,
the tribespeople, and cattle and goats and other domestic animals have learned to live in harmony under
Solomon Saibull's firm, but benevolent, stewardship.

The wild animals in Mr Saibull's care in the 2,000-
foot-deep Ngorongoro Crater he estimates in round
figures (without taking seasonal migrations of plains
game into account) as 5,000 zebra, 15,000 satyric
wildebeeste, 110 rhino (no headache in counting),
5,000 gazelles (divided between Grant's and Thomson's), 300–400 eland, 40 elephant (in the forest), 35
hippo, 80 lions, 70 kongoni and 400 hyena—apart
from buffalo, monkeys, and a number of other game
species like the sleek, swift water-buck.

How is it that Solomon Saibull finds himself the
chosen director of a big and vital pioneer venture in
shared land-usage which is being intently watched
by countries on other continents?

It is typical of his complete lack of hypocrisy or
pomposity that he claims no dramatic inner "call"
to the task nor advances any sentimental reasons for
accepting it. But his dedication is expressed in deeds.

His first visit to Ngorongoro was as a teenager, with
a party of classmates from the Lutheran Secondary
School, Arusha. It is surprising he ever wanted to set
eyes again on this famous spectacle. At that time there
were no roads into the Crater and "we had to struggle
down to its floor and up again". The double trip—
on a narrow, rocky road with a sheer, sickening drop
on one side—is terrifying enough in a Land-Rover
travelling in a low-ratio gear, but, at least, there is

little to fear from snakes and denizens as on foot.
Despite the enforced ordeal of his school "treat", Mr.
Saibull comments sincerely: "I was most impressed."

The road up to Ngorongoro from the lowlands, like
life itself tricky and treacherous now and then, began
for him many years before this schoolboy experience.

He was born just outside Arusha, among the green
hills of Africa and a hundred miles from the Crater
which is surrounded by the bones and relics of Man's
beginnings. His nomadic grandfather had moved with
his family to Arusha during the Great Famine,
caused by drought, of 1890–93 when thousands of
people and stock animals perished. As his parents
were inclined to settle (in one area near Arusha), the
young Saibull was sent to school. At the same time,
he was obliged to follow as fully as possible the main
customs of the tribe.

"I belonged to two worlds even at a fairly early age.
I was in a Christian school with a Christian name, and
yet I had to take part in the Masai rites for young men.

"With a group, I was given a symbolic father. During
the holidays, I had to strip off my school clothes and go
off alone into the bush. It was part of the toughening-up
process for manhood.

"The initiate has to sleep out in the open among dangerous animals. He has to be able to defend himself,
without a firearm of any sort, against a lion, if necessary.

"Before you apply to the "father" of your group to become a warrior (moran), you must be able to show him
you are able to take the place of one of the outgoing
moran. They have a good, carefree life and are generally
not keen to give it up. So you have to battle, literally.
You have to be able to fight a warrior, with staves as the
weapons, to win. There's nothing gentle like punching.
Masai boys are not allowed to punch: only the girls can
use their fists.

"You are obliged to demonstrate your courage in every possible way until all in your age group have proved they are ready for the next step.

"This is the circumcision ceremony, held at seven-year intervals by the Masai of Tanzania and Kenya. Under the knife, you must not give the slightest sign of fear or pain—not even blink an eyelid throughout the whole operation. And beforehand you are constantly and deliberately insulted by others of the tribe who yell "Coward", and worse, and try to make you crack up before the actual suffering ahead.

"The operation, however, does not make one a warrior, but the newly-circumcised has reached the *sipolio* stage. It is the last before the ceremony of becoming a *moran*, and lasts only a month, instead of six to nine months, if the candidate is, as I was, at school. And I did not have to wear the two black ostrich feathers in my hair, the blackened cloth, chalk all over my body and white facial designs which distinguish the warrior-to-be. But, with the others about to become *moran*, I was fed the blood of cattle mixed with milk. A lot of milk and very little blood. This mixture, while regarded by my people as beneficial in a number of ways, is by no means as widely used by the Masai as generally believed. For us in the *sipolio* category it is supposed to be a tonic; for a *moran* wounded in battle it was given as a form of transfusion. I once tried to drink warm blood which had been drawn from the vein of a cow. I didn't like it. Some of the Masai women who have to drink it to aid recovery after childbirth can only bring themselves to swallow it in the dark."

On the day the Masai youth becomes a warrior in the records of the tribe, he is washed and shaved from head to foot. All his clothing is thrown away, and he is given a new Masai name.

"I went through all that," said the Conservator. "You have to lose everything you can of your previous life. It's a kind of baptism. After that, you are a young *moran* between, say, 20 and 30. I was a warrior at 22, and will remain one for another two or three years. Then I became an elder."

He laughed and added: "Meanwhile, by custom, I am expected not to eat any meal prepared, seen or even touched by a woman. I am supposed to always eat and drink with another *moran.*"

After being received into the Masai warriors' ranks, Solomon Saibull left high school (he had begun his education at the age of nine) and studied mathematics, English, history and political science at Makerere University College in Kampala. Subsequently, he studied law for two years at the University of Exeter, and returned to his homeland to join the Ministry of External Affiairs in Dar-es-Salaam as Assistant Secretary.

"I didn't plan to go into any department of the Government connected with fauna and flora," he told me. "It just happened in a haphazard sort of way."

"The Ministry of Lands, Forests and Wildlife was very short of staff so I went there on loan for nine months. At the end of my sit-in in 1963, I was asked to go to Ngorongoro for four months as the white Conservator was on leave in England. My schedule in the Ministry had included matters concerning national parks, game reserves, and the Ngorongoro Conservation Area.

"I realised then that the people living there had to be developed with the help of the area's resources and at the same time the tremendous value of the area to the rest of the nation, and to mankind for recreation and research, had to be safeguarded."

He was appointed Conservator in September, 1965. He has a force of Masai-speaking guards and guides trained in forestry, game conservation and veterinary work.

Although, as in the rest of the gazetted Conservation Area, the Masai have been living in the Ngorongoro Crater for many generations, their presence in it is restricted to three villages and permits are renewable periodically to stop infiltration. Not being habitual meat eaters the Masai do not kill wild animals for food.

The men of Mr. Saibull's Conservation Unit take game counts; give lectures and film shows on the importance of the care of game and of possessing smaller, but higher quality, cattle herds; carry out research on rinderpest and other cattle plagues, and study the migration habits of the wild animals in the Crater which measures ten miles across from rim to rim. Water is piped from a spring to Masai on the rim to give them no excuse for entering the Crater with their cattle.

A year or so ago, President Nyerere personally vetoed a £15,000 project to build a "Treetops" type of hotel for tourists on the floor of the Crater. He feared animals would be scared off or disturbed, and a handsome new lodge has now been built up on the rim.

I spent several keenly-enjoyable hours touring the Crater with Mr. Saibull, and recalled my previous visit in late 1961 when he was still at university and the floor was bare and dusty in a severe drought (it now has a large lake with flamingos, and an all-weather airstrip). British civil servants, with the omniscience of their kind, informed me then that the total game population for all species in the Crater was no more than 8,000. It is happily clear today that they were well below the mark on the credit side, but the situation had been particularly depressing at that time. Apart from the ravages of the drought, the Masai were bringing increasing numbers of cattle into the Crater and had invaded the forests around the rim. The Governor of the day, Sir Richard Turnbull, called for a system that would enlist the full confidence and co-operation of the Masai and at the same time ensure conservation of both the game and the habitat. The peaceful co-existence between wild animals and the Masai ("The African farmer is not a brutal, bloodthirsty character, but is fighting a desperate battle with a harsh and grudging soil," said the Governor) which Sir Richard envisaged has been brought into being under President Nyerere's rule.

At the side of the man who is a chief character, I saw a good deal that memorable day of a progressive new chapter in the timeless story of that colossal, sun-swept crucible.

"We try to embrace everything in the Conservation Area," said Mr. Saibull. "After all, without the trees and the grasses there can be no elephant, rhino and zebra nor lion and cheetah and wild dogs."

We started out from the humble stone cottage among tall gum trees which he occupies while at work within the Crater. After a mile or so, he directed the Land-Rover driver to a patch of sunlight in which were two kittenish lionesses and a battle-scarred male. They were mating, but we were able to park but a few feet away from the trio, all in fine fettle.

"Don't ask me to stand up to them," said the Conservator as he leaned, smiling broadly, out of the front-seat window. "Here's one Masai that's not going to do that to a lion. . . . Why, one day I was about three hundred yards away from my vehicle, looking at a pool, when one of my chaps called and made signs that there were five lions in the reeds. It seemed a long, long way back to the Land-Rover, but they swear I covered the distance in a few seconds. Some people believe in 'freezing' on the spot and trying to out-stare a big animal. I just turn tail and run—like the evening when I was walking home here and looked up, after being deep in thought with my head bowed, just in time to save myself from colliding with a bull elephant blocking the path. I'd gone before it had a chance to stare at *me*."

Amiable and lucid, he is bi-lingual in English and his country's official language, Swahili.

One might even call the Conservator "tri-lingual", but in the strangest context. That high noon I heard him talk to the lions crouched around us. Peering out, he issued a series of powerful, deep-throated grunts and beguiling whines which so remarkably simulated those we had heard the animals themselves making in their courtship ecstasy. The lions responded—with cocked ears, amber stares, heads to one side, and rumblings which might have been entire sentences. I did not ask Mr. Saibull to translate. For his part, he merely explained that one of the lionesses was an intruder, and that the zebra and wildebeeste all around knew they were safe because a male lion will not allow the female to leave him and go off hunting while they are mating.

Although poaching is not now a heavy problem in the Conservation Area, the Conservator and his teams have to contend with trappers of baboons (which are surreptitiously smuggled out of the country to be sold for medical research or to zoos abroad) and ivory poachers out to bag elephants with hunter's rifles.

"Another type of poacher here catches buffalo in

hawser snares. It might be days before they arrive
to shoot their mutilated and agonised catch. And the
other week I caught a man baiting a leopard trap in
the fork of a tree with a gazelle he had poached."

Threats to Mr. Saibull's life, however, have not
come from poachers but Masai villagers who have
had to be re-settled.

"One particular incident was very frightening,"
he said. "It had been decided that it was necessary
to clear a nearby small crater of all human habitation so that its natural resources could be rehabili-
tated. The Masai clan there were given ample warning to go to another district. They consistently refused
to leave. After months and weeks had gone by, I went
over to try and reason with them. They wouldn't
listen to a word. Waving their war spears and long
knives, they surrounded me and shouted 'You will die
here', 'Your body will not leave this ground' and
similar unpleasant things. I managed to break away,
but in the end we had to call in a squad of the armed
Police Field Force to enforce the move."

Mr. Saibull has firm views on the pattern and roles
of national parks, springing from his consciousness of
how the animals in them can help to give under-
privileged humans, like so many of his fellow country-
men, a high standard of living.

"A nature park is preserved by Man for Man since
without him it is without significance to Man," he
says. "At the same time the presence of Man in a
nature park tends to destroy the qualities which he
wishes to preserve. A conflict is inevitable. Just as a
species has a right to struggle for survival, so has
Man. If, in order to survive, Man must destroy other
species, he will be entitled to do so. Similarly, if Man
must save other species for his own survival, he will

Watched by Tanzania's President Julius Nyerere, Emperor Haile Selassie (in uniform) feeds a young gazelle.

Tanzania Information Services

Zebra gallop along a dirt road in the Serengeti National Park in Tanzania.

Marion Kaplan

A young West African green vervet monkey in the Gambia's little
Abuko Nature Reserve.

not hesitate to preserve them. The task for the conservationist, therefore, is to make Man realise that he needs Nature for his own survival. If he succeeds, opposition to conservation methods will dwindle and die away."

Anticipating a five-fold rise on a shrinking globe in the number of tourists visiting East Africa from 1961 to 1971 (in 1963 the Ngorongoro Crater drew 11,000 visitors, in 1968 32,000), Mr. Saibull points a warning finger at the signs of "over-use" in some of Africa's national parks—too many tracks and roads, too many buildings and other objects foreign to the game. Backed by other African experts, he fears "complete spoliation" of some as a result of tourist invasions unless hotels and motels are sited just outside the parks, providing golf, tennis, dance halls, film shows, coffee shops, laundries, garages, chemists and hairdressers.

"Park towns just outside the main gate seem to be the answer. And these can stimulate local industry, whether it be in the form of crafts and farm products or direct employment. These places will open up areas which previously had been unable to take full advantage of the tourist trade passing before their eyes.

"The cardinal point is that the park should remain virtually unimpaired, and the animals left undisturbed. Nature should be hurt as little as possible. It is for this reason that it is necessary to anticipate increased visitor impact on nature parks and to plan for it well in advance. One way of doing so is to limit and spread out tourist facilities within the parks while accommodation must be located in suitable areas just outside."

The late afternoon shadows in the Crater lengthened as we rolled and lurched from one group of

L

animals to another, and files of Masai, their spears gleaming, were making their way across the hard ground to huddles of box-like huts.

We stopped a while to stretch our legs, and talked of a long letter in the local newspaper from a European who stated categorically that Africans were indifferent to the wonders of unspoilt Nature.

"I disagree with him in every respect," said the Conservator gently. "I know a large number of Africans who appreciate not only the economics of wildlife preservation, but also the intangible values of natural qualities. These are people—Africans—who can sit and watch Nature as it manifests itself in different subtle ways. The setting sun over the mauve hills, the lush scenery and the landscapes of rivers and valleys, the variety and abundance of creatures in their entire freedom—all forming a multitude of fascinating phenomena. Surely this rather fine feeling is not confined to Europe and America?"

Its white beard streaming, a wildebeeste galloped by.

"The power to appreciate Nature is very close to religious belief and, like faith, is universal," he remarked as we climbed back into the Land-Rover.

A Quintet of Custodians

Set in extensive grounds which have all the splendour of botanical gardens, Makerere University College on the slope of one of Kampala's Hills has produced more than its fair complement of Africans who have become prominent in the running of their country.

Two of them—the men who are the heads of wild animal protection in Uganda, legendary home of Rider Haggard's *She*, and among Africa's foremost countries in conservation—now have their headquarters within the shadow of Makerere.

They are balding Sylvester Ruhweza, Chief Game Warden of the Republic's progressive Game Department who was chairman of the committee which drew up the O.A.U.'s deed for the preservation of Nature (see final chapter), and handsome, urbane Francis Katete, 36-year-old Director of National Parks.

Mr. Ruhweza, aged 42, is married, and the father of six children. After attending a secondary school and a college in his homeland, he went to Makerere where he studied physics, natural science and chemistry. He was a schoolmaster in Kampala and his home area of Fort Portal for a number of years until he obtained a scholarship to take a course in zoology at the University of Wales.

Returning to Uganda, he again taught for a while; then became a biologist in the Ministry of Animal Industry, Game and Fisheries. In 1963 he was among those chosen by the American Government to study game management in the States through a number of departments there. He returned to his job as a biologist, but in 1964 he was appointed a senior game warden under an expatriate and held this appointment until 1966 when he became Uganda's Chief Game Warden.

Mr. Ruhweza admits his interest in animals developed slowly, but it is clear he is now an ardent and active conservationist who likes to get away from his desk and paper work and out into the country as much as possible.

He defines his responsibilities as "preserving wild life, coping with problems of ecology, studying the changing pattern of land use, and advising the Government".

Although some 500 poachers are brought to court every year in Uganda and 5–6,000 snaring devices are destroyed annually, Mr. Ruhweza feels that the situation is sometimes magnified and misunderstood outside Africa.

"People have lived with animals since time began," he says, "and every Ugandan has the right to meat. To cope with this traditional view, we have a policy of selling the meat of cropped animals to the poor for a few pence a pound."

African children in Kampala and other urban

regions may never see game so a zoo is maintained at Entebbe, where Mr. Ruhweza is stationed, for educational purposes as well as caring for sick, orphaned or aged wild animals.

Checking the presence, distribution and thin ranks of the black rhino and the mountain gorilla is a constant task of Uganda Game Department officials.

Under Chief Warden Ruhweza, they are responsible for three different types of areas:

(a) Fifteen game reserves where no other form of land use is accepted. There were only three at independence, and these reserves do not include the country's three national parks. Some hunting, under licence, is allowed in the reserves.

(b) Eight sanctuaries where all, or some, species are protected but are not free from land use.

(c) Controlled hunting areas.

"And yet safari organisers are always pleading with me for other hunting areas where they claim the game are more plentiful," he said. "I have one answer to all these requests: my duty is not to hand over animals for money, but to try to keep them in existence."

Nevertheless, the Game Department, while fulfilling its functions of conservation and education, is still able to make a profit from the issue of hunting licences (£50 for an elephant), the sale of trophies, entrance fees to parks and reserves, and sales of game meat. In the year 1967–68, the Government spent £92,000 on projects related to game for a return of £155,000. In the year 1968–69 the outlay was £100,000 and the return will be proportionately higher.

I found Mr. Ruhweza, who in 1969 presented

certificates to successful students at the latest graduation ceremony at the College of African Wildlife
Management in Tanzania, distressed by an American
magazine writer who had suggested that colonies of
chimpanzees deep in Budongo, a tropical jungle in
north-west Uganda, might soon be threatened because wild fig trees, a source of food for some animals
but useless commercially, were being weeded out by
poison as part of a timber exploitation scheme.

It was explained to me by him and a senior official
of the Forest Conservation Department in Entebbe
that (1) the slow process of making the scheduled,
thickly-wooded 140 square miles of Budongo an economic project, with planting and controlled felling,
would take half-a-century to achieve; (2) some 136
square miles of surrounding, open forest, including
fig trees, would be untouched; (3) even in the spots
where they were poisoned, the fig trees, prolific
breeders, would regenerate; (4) the chimpanzees did
not live on wild figs alone, and (5) were the chimps
in danger (which Mr. Ruhweza vigorously denied),
there would be no necessity to create a reserve for
them in Budongo for the forest extended into Murchison Falls National Park a few miles away.

On this ever-burning question concerning the conflict between the interests of people, or economics,
and animals, the chief of parks, Francis Katete, a
BSc, asked: "How does one distinguish between
them? If Murchison Falls Park did not exist, 600
people, who in turn support large numbers of de-
pendants, would lose their jobs."

He said in his office in Kampala: "We live in a
world of inter-dependence between Man and his environment, which consists of plants and animals and
land. You just cannot draw lines like that. The very

preservation of wild animals is in the human interest.

"The animals are part of my country. You knock them out and you will mutilate Uganda, as if you were cutting off a limb."

Director Katete was born near Kampala, the son of "a simple farmer". He went to primary school in the area of his village, and then to college. Subsequently, he read botany and zoology at Makerere.

"It was then that I became especially interested in animals. Towards the last year at Makerere, my course took us out into the field and we spent some time in one of the national parks. I came to know more about wild life, and I felt I would be interested in working with a wild life set up. When I finished my degree, there was an opening, and I went in as a game ranger. That was nine years ago.

"I spent a year in London studying conservation and ecology at University College. When I came back to the Game Department, I started an education and publicity scheme—touring schools and telling people what game conservation was in the Ugandan context.

"I then worked in the field for some time. When the Department of National Parks wanted a Deputy Director, I applied, and ended up in 1964 as Director of Parks."

He has a nation-wide staff of 800, from wardens down to porters. The parks of which he is overseer are some of the most attractive in Africa, crowded with elephant and buffalo. They cover about three per cent of the total surface area of Uganda which has also managed to be a generous host, providing land, camp staffs and transport, to legions of homeless men, women and children—refugees from the long civil

strife in southern Sudan, and from Rwanda, the
Congo and Burundi.

"The parks contribute more than three per cent of
the gross income of the country," says Mr. Katete.
"Since tourism is buoyantly increasing, we can expect
that in time the parks will provide considerably more
than their share towards national income."

The Director spells out his version of the objectives
of a national park as "the protection and propagation
in as natural a state as possible of animal and vegetable life; the protection of geological, archaeological,
historical and aesthetic features and any object of
scientific interest, and the study of such objects for
the benefit, education and enjoyment of visitors".

On the question of charging park entrance fees to
residents and tourists alike, he maintains: "It would
be difficult to attach a figure to the total enjoyment,
refreshments, experience and excitement in the case
of children and other people who have not seen con-
centrations of wild animals. What price do you attach
to this sense of excitement, and the addition to a person's store of knowledge? By my way of thinking,
national parks have a human value to which you
cannot attach a price."

Asked if he agreed that national parks should be
run exclusively as economic assets, he replied:
"Human values are difficult to measure in terms of
profit and loss."

Mr. Katete would like to see set aside "defined
areas which are carefully and scientifically managed",
or where surplus game populations have to be reduced, to provide animals for sportsmen.

"I may not enjoy seeing an elephant shot dead,
but some people enjoy doing this and are prepared
to pay for it."

An implacable enemy of poachers, he wants better armed, better trained rangers to be able to safeguard themselves against deadly attacks by gangs of lawless hunters.

Learning at the time of my visit to him of a rhino killing by ivory poachers who were aided by a band of villagers, the Director issued an anguished statement to the Press and radio and TV networks of Uganda. It read: "When will the people come to realise that their participation in the nefarious trade of rhino horns is destructive to themselves and their cultural heritage?"

At Murchison Falls National Park there is a bespectacled, ex-city man "now in love with Nature" who feels just as strongly about poachers—Ponsiano Ssemwezi, at 40 a senior warden.

A married man with two children, Mr. Ssemwezi was also born near Kampala and first became interested in wild animals when he was studying zoology, botany and geography at Makerere. He obtained a diploma in education, and became a schoolteacher for eight years.

In 1966, he was put in charge of wild life educa tion at Murchison Falls.

It is a hard, full-time job for a remote corner of Africa. In addition to his other duties, Mr. Ssemwezi is in charge of the Wildlife Education Centre at Murchison where three groups of buildings, within a hundred yards of each other, symbolise development there.

The first is a grass-thatched mud hut, the original centre, which is now falling apart but is allowed to remain to illustrate progress. The second is the modern centre, containing the exhibits and lecture room and built in stone and wood with a decorative tiled roof; and thirdly, the dormitory. This consists of a gaggle of prefabricated huts, with tin roofs, which are being replaced as funds become available.

In the year after his appointment, Ponsiano Ssemwezi had 3,473 visitors to the Murchison education centre, largely schoolchildren of all ages and levels.

There are regular visits of parties of African boys and girls from all over Uganda, accompanied by their teachers. Those who have travelled long distances are put up in the dormitory huts and provided with hot meals.

This is a typical day in the education warden's life: Up at dawn to organise and take part in a tour of the park with a large party of primary schoolchildren. The convoy of mini-buses stops every few minutes for him to tell the children about each animal or flower spotted. The tour is followed by a launch trip on the Victoria Nile, viewing crocodile and hippo. A teachers' association arrives on the group's return late in the afternoon, and at nine that night he gives the adults a talk on the park and game conservation in general.

The next morning he may be preparing for another three-hour tour of the park with a new batch of children, or joining other wardens in an emergency situation like a massed strike against poachers or helping to control a bush or forest fire.

"Fires are sometimes as big a threat as poaching," he said.

And with "sidelines" to assist in such as game counts and the periodic, nominal cropping of hippo on the river bank, he has little time for his hobby— bird watching.

Director Katete's counterpart in next-door Kenya is burly Perez Olindo who, in his early thirties, is outstanding among new Africa's youngest, brightest and best-qualified public servants of high rank concerned with wild life.

An expert zoologist and biologist, a devoted and talented official and a family man, Mr. Olindo has a dozen national parks, ranging from 44 square miles to 41,800 acres, under his control in Kenya where African schoolchildren run their own "Save the Game" clubs.

Born in the Kakamega district of western Kenya, he became a teacher on leaving high school. During 1960 he attended Central Missouri State College in Warrensburg for initial training in game control. He was there for two years, and then spent the next two years at Michigan State University from which he emerged with BSc in zoology (wild life management).

"Back in Kenya, I joined the Game Department as a biologist. Because of a staff shortage, I was later transferred to the Coast Province, south of Malindi, as a game warden."

Mr. Olindo was switched to the Department of National Parks in 1965 to understudy the white Director and well-known game authority, Colonel Mervyn H. Cowie, who resigned early in 1966. Cowie was succeeded by his African deputy who has held the post ever since.

In his job he has to be, he says, "a flyer, a driver and a walker". He is a qualified pilot, having learned at Wilson Airport next to Nairobi National Park, and he can fly any one of the Department's six light planes which are used on anti-poaching patrols, game counts and fire control.

"A plane is most useful for my consultation and inspection trips to various parks which would otherwise take many hours."

His original ambition was to enter the realm of medicine, but an American teacher at his high school at Kakamega put him in touch with a pen friend at Michigan State University and from this correspondence his concern for animals developed.

Mr. Olindo has two children, a three-year-old girl named Sable and a baby boy named Bongo.

"Calling them after antelope species was the idea of my wife, Kate. Our families and friends sometimes tease us about it, but we are used to all that now. We think they are rather nice names."

The Olindo family live in a pleasant house only a mile away from Nairobi National Park where in 1969 handsome Hassan Said Mohammed became its first African warden-in-charge.

Mr. Mohammed is typical of many of the park rangers now under him, binocular-sighted men like so many of their colleagues all over Africa who work long hours days and night, and pluckily track lion and elephant and rhino on foot or their bicycles in order to be able to tell visitors each day where particular animals can be found.

He started in the game conservation service more than 20 years ago as a ranger in a reserve of 11,000 square miles. "I was born with animals, and lived with them all my life."

At the beginning of the sixties, he worked in Tsavo National Park. He took part in campaigns against poachers, and carried out research work.

After a study tour of America, he was admitted to the College of Wildlife Management, and at the end of two years' training there he was appointed warden of Kenya's newly-gazetted Lake Nakuru National Park.

Under Mr. Mohammed's jurisdiction, and situated

at the main entrance to the Nairobi National Park, is a chapel-like building which houses a wild life education centre similar to that, with the exception of a dormitory, at Murchison. It includes a visual aids section, a lecture room, and a small, but well-equipped, museum devoted to the theme of the care of wild animals. Hundreds of thousands of pupils from Kenya African schools have visited the centre since it was opened in June, 1965.

Talks on game conservation are given there to groups of children by uniformed African rangers, and documentary films on the subject, with Swahili commentaries, are shown.

Mr. Mohammed feels the narrowest escape from a wild animal he has had during his long period of employment in the parks was in Tsavo some years ago.

"We were trying to establish the migration patterns of elephants by spraying paint on their bottoms. Our equipment consisted of a gas cylinder with a long pipe attached through which the paint spurted when we set the thing off.

"One evening we stopped very close to a waterhole. We had just got set up when a herd came along. Suddenly a big, bad-tempered female saw this pipe and began to investigate. It followed the pipe, right up to me. As I was thinking—rooted to the spot—that this was the end and waited to be trampled to death, the warden with whom I was working sprang up and shouted at the old girl.

"She hesitated for a few chilly seconds, then turned and ambled off back to the herd."

Father of six children, Mr. Mohammed says: "I hope one of them will take my place one day."

"Animal Interpol"

An epochal chapter in the story of the protection of wild life in independent Africa was written in the first quarter of 1969.

After a week's conference which was the first of its kind, the representatives of five States, supported by two other nations, drew up a blueprint of co-operation in the conservation of game animals.

The unique forum was the brain-child of Perez Olindo. He also introduced a welcome break with colonial tradition in that the talks were held out in the bush among the animals instead of in a stuffy urban hall.

The delegates—senior African officials and wardens in the national parks and game departments of Uganda, Ethiopia, Kenya, Somalia and Tanzania, backed by Zambia and Malawi—spent their time keenly deliberating, researching, exploring and living among the game herds in both the western and eastern sections of Tsavo National Park—in which London would be swallowed up.

Elephant, buffalo, rhino, giraffe, and lion (whose ancestors in the locality dragged coolie workers from carriages and the track and devoured them on the spot during the turn-of-the-century building of the "Iron Snake" railway from Mombasa to Lake Victoria) roamed the valleys and plains of Tsavo as the visitors debated the future all over Africa of such creatures.

They were told how the animals around them had descended from the once-teeming populations, originally severely reduced for skins, ivory, food or by way of plain protection by the Arab slave-traders whose caravans followed the Galana River from the coast to the hinterland and returned with heartbreak processions of chained and whip-lashed captives.

The railway, which opened up East Africa to white colonisation and on which a young lion-hunter named Winston Churchill travelled on the engine's cow-catcher, brought with it pioneers, prospectors, big-game sportsmen and poachers, all of whom took a heavy toll of the crowded gamelands.

But Tsavo's 600,000,000-year-old terrain of red earth, marbled and granitic rock, lava cones and prickly trees remains unchanged, and one of its many grand and fascinating features seen by the conference delegates was Mudanda Rock, a whale-back outcrop nearly a mile long which directs each shower of rain into a pool beneath. In dry weather, hundreds of elephant come from miles around to drink and bathe. By the time they arrive, each is covered in dust and is as red as a blush. They leave in line ahead, grey, glistening and refreshed. Visits were also made to Mzima Springs where the men gazed from a wooden jetty into a sun-dappled pool where hippo, crocodile and shoals of barbel could be clearly seen.

Eight miles from this idyllic spot is Kilaguni, a large stone and timber lodge with roofs made from matted palm-leaves, where the conservationists stayed for the first half of the conference. Mount Kilimanjaro, with its great snow-cap glimmering in the sun, looms over Kilaguni like a mirage high above the clouds. The lodge has its own airstrip (over which planes may have to circle while elephant are driven off), and a bar where a bold notice requests the guests to be quiet while the animals are drinking!

Literally at the visitor's feet on the long, open verandah at most times of the day and night are dozens of elephant, buck and zebra. So accustomed to human beings have the animals and birds become that Kilaguni might be the home of Dr. Doolittle.

Having tea on the terrace, one is visited out of the sky by a fearless company of quaint hornbills, electric-blue starlings looking like flying jewels, and perky yellow weaver birds, all of which jostle on the tray to dip their beaks into the sugar bowl and the milk jug. And, as the elephants stare in Olympian reproach from a few yards away, the birds gobble up the crumbs of cake and cucumber sandwiches.

The headquarters for the second half of the talks was the new and Government-sponsored Voi Safari Lodge, set high on a hillside in Tsavo East where there are nearly sixty types of mammal. In each bedroom, the tourist has the breathtaking sensation of looking out of the window of an aircraft flying low over the vast plain, studded with bushes and stunted acacias.

A hundred miles from Mombasa and 210 miles from Nairobi, the Voi Lodge—built, like its swimming pool, into living rock—is among the forerunners of a novel luxury type in rugged parts of Africa. While in character with its dramatic site, the timbered lodge provides modern, international standards of food, comfort and service comparable with those of a first-class city hotel.

In baker's oven temperatures, there is ice galore. Small carved African masks form the door-handles of the fifty double bedrooms which have private bathrooms, points for electric razors and patterned African cloths on the walls.

Clusters of gourds provide the shades for electric-light bulbs of soft yellow in the bar and lounge. The chalet-style dining room, the balconies and a specially constructed observation platform overlook a natural water-hole at which elephant and other animals can be seen drinking by day, and by flood-light at night.

Discussions throughout the conference at both sites followed four main themes:

1. The place of wild life in the general context of good land use. This question arises from the virtual impossibility of creating a national park or reserve as a self-appointed unit. All wild life areas depend to some extent on the areas nearby and can be adversely affected by industrialisation and agricultural schemes, cattle ranching, the hydro-electric development around—and, even as can happen, inside—them. The conference examined in detail different solutions to the problems of managing game areas in association with other forms of land use.

2. The impact of tourism on wild life. While parks are created to preserve the wild animals, tourism (although it would not dry up even without game in outstandingly attractive countries, or those with a wonder of the world like Victoria Falls, such as Malawi, Zambia, Ghana, Kenya, and others) provides their main economic justification. Tourist development, in fact, conflicts sometimes with the best interests of wild life management. The

M

conference hammered out some guidelines for the proper co-ordination of the two activities.

3. Wild life education. To survive, national parks need public support which can best be achieved by education, particularly where they exist in, or near, densely populated areas. The conference compared notes on various types of educational programmes to interest people of all races in Africa in wild animals and their preservation.

4. Poaching and allied problems. The control of poaching inside parks and other designated reserves is bound up with the control of dealings in trophies outside their boundaries and at international level. Some game herds may move across State boundaries or outside the control of a parks department. Provided with individual statistics on imported, transit and locally hunted trophies, such as leopard skins and ivory, delegates were able to see how these figures compared with the respective export figures.

Opening the conference, Kenya's Minister for Tourism and Wildlife said it had "a very special significance" in that it was the first time that those directly in charge of African national parks and game departments had come together on their own to discuss the many and varied problems which they had to face from day to day.

Mr. Olindo pointed out at the ceremony that the conference, which was built around committees of delegates who volunteered to be assigned to one or more of the four discussion topics, had the merit of at last allowing African officers in the field of animal conservation to make personal contact with their opposite numbers who were doing the same work in different countries and different surroundings. All the discussions, he said, were intended to assist in the formation of national and international game policies.

In the course of the talks, Mr. Ssemwezi of Murchison Falls National Park said that trained conservationists ought to visit African schools regularly. The radio and television should be increasingly used for conservation education outside the parks. Wild life educationists should prepare a book recommendable to schools in Africa as part of the programmes to teach the young the importance of game conservation.

"While anti-poaching measures must take a lion's share of the parks' budget, my impression is that it leaves almost nothing for wild life education," he added.

Tanzania's African chief game officer said that in his country controlled areas were being set aside in which the hunting of game was regulated in such a way that the ratio of cropping did not exceed the natural increase of any species.

One of the most important outcomes of the bush forum followed lengthy discussions on how to control the movement of illegal game trophies, particularly the skins of the large cats. At the time there was no common legislation between neighbouring States in Africa. But the delegates unanimously agreed that concerted action should be taken against poachers and other "dealers in death" with a tough form of "Animal Interpol". This involves game rangers, police and border guards of the five, or more, countries working together through their game ministries, and exchanging information on game-skin smugglers, non-licensed hunters, and animal snatchers for hole-in-the-wall zoos abroad.

"Grave concern" was expressed that international air regulations stipulated that the suitcases of a departing traveller need not be opened. Entry and

Exit checkpoints in trophy-producing countries were urged.

The African signatories to the Tsavo conference (representing nearly 60,000,000 people) have arranged with their governments for an exchange of black-lists of convicted trophy dealers and poachers between their respective countries.

They are pressing for stern deterrent sentences on a common basis for all offences connected with the reduction of game populations outside officially sanctioned scientific and culling schemes.

Photostat copies of documents used for the importation of jungle trophies, such as tusks or leopard skins, are now being exchanged from State to State; and it is hoped that mutual legislation will ensure mandatory declaration of each wild animal skin to cross inter-State borders.

The owners of an increasing number of abattoir-like curio shops in main centres, especially Nairobi, will be questioned from time to time on the exact circumstances of how they came to be in possession of some part of a wild animal from which a souvenir has been made. Late in 1969, Kenya Game Department officials raided a Nairobi curio store and temporarily confiscated £45,000 worth of trophies.

The setting up of State-run taxidermists as a monopoly in each country and stricter control of zoological specimens were recommended by the conference which was backed by the Rockefeller Brothers' Trust, the Ford Foundation and the African Wildlife Leadership Foundation of Washington (many men in key conservation positions in Africa today owe their careers to American funds and training).

The active participation of Ethiopia and Somalia in the "Animal Interpol" scheme, which, even in these early stages, is expected to reduce considerably the numbers of game killers over a large area of Africa, was particularly gratifying to conservation authorities on and outside the African continent.

At the time of the conference the Republic of Somalia had just enacted stringent new game laws to replace "The old and outdated ex-Italian and ex-British legislation".

Welcoming the delegates' decision to launch a combined all-out war on criminals of the wilds, Kenya's Minister of Tourism said it was not enough to take independent action in each country to control the illegal trade in game trophies "which gives rise to poaching and the indiscriminate destruction of wild animals." There *had* to be inter-State—in fact, international—co-ordination.

"As long as we are vigilant (note: in Uganda, Tanzania and Kenya units of the Army are sometimes used against poachers) and mutually co-operative, we should be able to crush much of the ghastly business of the killing and exploitation of wild things," said Convenor Olindo. "More and more African countries will join us in the common fight as time goes on."

The conference is to be an annual, and expanding, event, held in turn in each of the participant nations.

The Way Ahead

"Nowadays, many Africans, having expert knowledge, are dedicated to the cause of preservation. If only to be practical, they also realise the benefits obtained from tourist revenue. Pre-uhuru, the cry was raised that wild life would be sacrificed by independent governments caring nothing about the aesthetic values of their heritage. Like so many other doleful predictions, this fear has proved utterly baseless.

"Governments have excelled themselves in their conservation efforts, recognising not only the interests of their own countries but the duty they owe to the world in general to protect a geographical area which is one of the last remaining repositories on earth of wild life living in a natural state."—Editorial, *East African Standard*, April 1969.

What of the future in Africa?

A mass pledge has been given by the Heads of State that the animals are to be safeguarded on a Pan-African basis. In Algiers in September 1968 leaders of all independent nations in Africa not under white rule signed a bulky, historic document which, when the foregone individual ratification processes have

been completed in each contracting country during
this year, will be a beacon of its kind for the world.

This Organisation for African Unity charter re-
places the 1933 London Convention for the Conservation of Wildlife, the signatories to which were the
colonial powers whose tutelage of the animals has
been smoothly taken over by the rightful trustees.

Like its 36-year-old basic counterpart, the little
publicised African document, occupying several foolscap pages, is also called a "Convention", the pre-
amble to which states that "we accept our duty to
harness the natural and human resources of our Continent for the total advancement of our peoples in
spheres of human endeavour."

The Convention declares that the signatories are
"fully conscious of the ever-growing importance of
natural resources from economic, nutritional, scientific, educational, cultural and aesthetic points of view
. . . and of the dangers which threaten some of these
irreplaceable assets".

It lays down that the contracting States "shall
ensure conservation, wise use and development of
faunal resources and their environment within the
framework of land-use planning and of economic and
social development" and "shall manage aquatic
environment, whether in fresh, brackish or coastal
water, with a view to minimise deleterious effects of
any water and land use practice which might
adversely affect aquatic habitats".

They are obliged to adopt or maintain adequate
laws on hunting, capture and fishing under which the
issue of permits is properly regulated, and unauthor-
ised methods are prohibited.

The following means of hunting, capture and
fishing are prohibited under the new Convention—any

method liable to cause a mass destruction of wild animals; the use of drugs, poisons, poisoned weapons or poisoned baits; the use of explosives. The following methods are "more particularly prohibited"—the use of mechanically propelled vehicles except as authorised and controlled by the competent authority; the use of fire; the use of firearms capable of firing more than one round at each pull of the trigger; hunting or capture at night except as authorised and controlled by the competent authority; the use of missiles containing detonators.

The use of nets and stockades, concealed traps, pits, snares, set-gun traps, deadfalls and hunting from a blind or hide is to be "strictly controlled".

The foregoing represents the crime calendar for all Africa, including hunting in the dark by spotlight to hold an animal transfixed while it is shot down.

Another provision recognises that it is "important and urgent" to accord special protection to those animal species which are threatened with extinction, or which may become so, and to the habitat necessary to their survival. "Where such a species is represented only in the territory of one contracting State, that State has a peculiar responsibility for its protection."

There is a call for common action in regulating the traffic in animal specimens and trophies "which have been illegally captured or killed or obtained".

"Trophy" under the Convention means any dead animal specimen or part thereof included in a manufactured or processed object or otherwise, unless it has lost its original identity.

A "conservation area" is defined as "any protected natural resource area, whether it be a strict natural reserve, a national park or a special reserve".

A "strict natural reserve", according to the Convention, means an area under State control, the boundaries of which may not be altered nor any portion alienated except by the competent legislative authority (Parliament). In such a reserve, any form of hunting or fishing, any undertaking connected with forestry, agriculture or mining, any grazing, any excavation or prospecting, drilling, levelling of the ground or construction, any work tending to alter the configuration of the soil or the character of the vegetation, any water pollution and, generally, any act likely to harm or disturb the fauna, including the introduction of zoological species, whether indigenous or imported, wild or domesticated, are "strictly forbidden". Scientific investigations, including the removal of animals from "a strict natural reserve", may only be undertaken by special permission, and it is forbidden to fly at low altitude over such an area.

A "national park" is defined as an area under State control where, again, the boundaries may not be changed except by legislation. It is "exclusively set aside for the propagation, protection, conservation and management of vegetation and wild animals for the benefit and enjoyment of the general public". The killing, hunting and capture of animals there is banned "except for scientific and management purposes and on condition that such measures are taken under the direction or control of the competent authority".

The activities prohibited in a "strict natural reserve", including camping and settlement, may also be forbidden in a national park.

A "special reserve" means another protected area, such as a game reserve, which denotes an area set aside, in terms of the Convention, for the management and propagation of wild animal life and the protection and management of its habitat. The hunting, killing or capture of fauna is prohibited except by, or under the direction or control, of the reserve authorities. Settlement and other human activities are controlled or prohibited.

The Convention also refers to those parts of a country (a "partial reserve" or "sanctuary") set aside to protect characteristic wild life, or to protect a particularly threatened animal where "all other interests and activities shall be subordinated to this end".

It further declares: "The contracting States shall maintain, and extend where appropriate, within their territory, and where applicable in their territorial waters, the conservation areas existing at the time of entry into force of the present Convention and, preferably within the framework of land-use planning programmes, assess the necessity of establishing additional conservation areas in order to protect those ecosystems which are most representative of their territories and to ensure the conservation of all species."

In some countries, game conservation areas are now to be surrounded by non-hunting belts as extra protection; and African district councils or tribal authorities have designated their own preserves, deriving profit from the sale of permits to photograph or hunt game.

The signatories contracted to "encourage and promote research in conservation, utilisation and management of natural resources", and to "ensure that their peoples appreciate their close dependence on natural resources and understand the need, and rules for, the rational utilisation of these resources".

Full educational programmes and information campaigns "capable of acquainting the public with, and winning it over to, the idea of conservation" are urged.

The various States undertake to make maximum use of the educational value of each conservation area, and to ensure that wild life conservation and management of natural resources are treated as an integral part of national development plans.

Under this Game Charter of the O.A.U., there are "A" and "B" classes of heavily protected species. Throughout each land, the hunting, killing, capture or collection of those in Category "A" "shall be permitted only on the highest authority, and only if required in the national interest or for scientific purposes". Wild life in Class "B" may be hunted, killed, captured or collected only under special authorisation granted by the competent authority in any contracting State.

Additional or listed species may be placed in "A" or "B" by the country concerned, according to specific requirements commensurate with the degree of danger to them at a particular time.

Among the species in "A" category are the Golden Cat, all flamingos, the cheetah, marine turtles, the dugong and the manatee, and many other mammals and birds.

The Golden Cat, built like a leopard and with a long tail, is rarely seen except as a tawny flash in a forest clearing. It is about twice the size of the average tabby.

The cheetah, reputed to be the fastest animal on four legs with bursts of 60 m.p.h. or more (I once clocked one at 45 m.p.h. in a Land-Rover over 200 yards), is more of a dog than a cat. Its claws are blunt

and, unlike a feline, only partially sheathable. But it
has a deep-throated purr. The cheetah, which runs
down smaller gazelles over open country and seizes its
prey in its jaws at the throat, makes a handsome and
affectionate pet after being reared from a cub. The
cheetah is now rare in Africa (often being mistaken by
pelt poachers for a leopard), and is feared to have
vanished in India and the Near East.

The leathery marine turtle, or Luth, has a few
breeding beaches left on the west coast of Afrca.
They weigh more than half a ton when fully grown,
and have a nine-foot flipper span. Collection of its
eggs for commercial purposes has severely reduced
the species.

The long "B" list includes the giant forest hog,
the African lynx, the dwarf antelope, the aardvark,
Burchell's zebra, the Bongo, the situtunga or marsh
antelope, and—proving they do exist on the "steppes"
of Africa—the aardwolf.

The tusked giant forest hog, which is scattered
lightly over East and West Africa, is a hairy, black-
bristle monster which is terrifying in its headlong
rushes at an attacker. It has a fearsome, boar's scowl,
and was the quarry of pig-sticking expeditions by the
white *sahibs* in Africa's old days. In its wooded
haunts, the giant forest hog is sometimes marked
down in error as a young buffalo.

The nocturnal African lynx is a fierce, but attractive, wild feline. With tufts of dark hair growing from
the tips of its ears, it has a devilish appearance and
could well be a witch's cat. It is known in some parts
of Africa as the Caracal. They sometimes attack a
roosting eagle for a meal, or a sitting ostrich if particularly ravenous.

The dwarf antelope is a living miniature Bambi,

and the smallest of the species. It has liquid brown
eyes, tiny horns and a shaggy grey and light-brown
coat. It lives in clumps of bushes or areas of woodland, and exudes a scent of musk from facial glands
when startled and plunging from its hide-out.

A "nightmare bear" (I once saw one, covered in
red mud, crossing a main road at night in Kenya and
in the headlights it looked like a wallaby conjured up
by LSD) might be an apt description for the aardvark, or ant-bear. It has bear-like claws for digging,
but any resemblance to the real grizzly ends right
there. It has a long, pig-like snout and a sticky, whip-
like tongue which is inserted into termite hills for food
in the night.

The extinct Quagga, of which the last specimen
was seen in South Africa in 1878, is thought to have
been the most southerly relative of Burchell's zebra
which looks like a circus pony painted with black
stripes. It has a hoarse call, and wanders the plains
in tightly-knit herds on the not too successful safety-
in-numbers defence plan against hunting lions.

The quaintly named Bongo is a heavy, eland-like
brown antelope with fearsome horns, and a white
strip on the bridge of its nose. Some of its last refuges
are in isolated parts of both East and West Africa.

The hyena-type aardwolf feeds, like the more
grotesque ant-bear, on large colonies of termites. Its
diet, which makes it more popular to human beings
than its shifty appearance would otherwise warrant,
also consists of the rodents which carry bubonic
plague. When alarmed, it raises a cape of coarse hairs
on its back. It then looks twice its size.

There is ample evidence that all black States with
anything left to offer on hoof and wing are fervently

agreed on the priorities of survival for the creatures of the jungle, bush and savannah.

It is heartening to record that, in large measure, the retreat of wild animals has been held; and it is Africans who have stemmed the drain in blood and bone.

Efforts being directed to the encouragement of participation by African tribesmen in the protection of the national parks and game reserves are slowly bearing fruit, especially now the admonitions regarding conservation are expressed by their own people at the top and not some expatriate white *baas*.

The ranks of animal lovers in the African nations become greater with enlightenment, and with every new generation.

An African administrator claims that his people have always had a deep, latent feeling for animals, adding: "The best expression of this is in a rich folklore, full of charming stories. With education comes a deeper interest, and consciousness of a national heritage."

But having had to live his own tooth-and-claw existence during the course of a rugged upbringing, not every ordinary African is as yet a natural sentimentalist about wild life, appreciating both its beauty and value.

It is plain, however, that a steadily rising number among scores of millions are determined that their sweeping game sanctuaries from the Sahara to the Zambezi shall not wither and die.

Epilogue

In this book, I have swung a broad spotlight across the animal realms of mid-Africa.

Here now, for tomorrow's far-reaching traveller of modest means who will join the low-cost, mass flights to this Continent, the beam is narrowed to focus on some of the star game sanctuaries, as regards the beauty of their settings and the abundance or variety of their inhabitants, which have not yet been mentioned in detail.

The list—but a token guide—also notes one or two hitherto unpublicised protection areas now being brought into existence as whole-hearted attempts are made to draw certain lesser-known animals back from the brink of oblivion. Such new havens are the order of the hour throughout Africa.

Botswana

Chobe Reserve (in the green northern part of this country which is the size of France): Large herds of elephant; lion families; leopards; black rhino; buffalo; sable antelope; eland; kudu; waterbuck;

171

ostrich; zebra; impala; Chobe bushbuck, giraffe and gemsbok, or oryx.

Notes: Three or four years ago, United Nations' ecologists maintained this lowly nation contained "the largest concentration of plains game in Africa". It is President Khama's aim to keep it that way, and his current Five Year Plan provides for a buoyant tourist industry, based on this broad spectrum of wild animals, and for the building of well-appointed hotels and tourist lodges. These are to be owned or managed by Africans who will also run photographic and hunting safaris.

Black-mane lions are to be found in the Ngamiland controlled hunting area.

One tribe maintains its own 700-square-mile wild life reserve called Moremi. There are rare species of gazelle to be found in this energetically protected tract of forest, desert and swamp as well as lion, rhino, elephant and leopard. While the animals are conserved, fee-paying tourists help to fill the tribal coffers. The graceful klipspringer antelope, the giraffe and the cheetah are among the animals declared Royal game in this country.

Ethiopia

Awash National Park (800 square miles) is newly established, and the first of its kind in the "Land of Sheba". It is within easy driving distance of Addis Ababa, the capital, and has a good selection of game such as cheetah, gazelles, leopard and elephant. The latter were re-introduced to the area.

Notes: Game wardens are stationed in several lonely areas of this rugged land to protect wild animals and two more national parks are being created. One is set in a rugged mountain area exceeding the Grand Canyon in its grandeur, and the principal species it will safeguard are the Abyssinian wolf (otherwise known as the Simien fox), the Walia Ibex, and the Gelada baboon. The disappearing Walia Ibex had been gravely threatened in the district by poachers using old Italian military rifles and tribespeople rolling boulders down cliff faces on to the antelope-type animal. It is stoutly built as a supply of meat, and has massive horns.

The Nyala antelope is protected in another mountainous district.

Thirty-five species, including the Colobus monkey whose numbers have been so grievously reduced in the past to provide rugs and other decorations, are now classified Royal game, and special permits— rarely granted—are needed to hunt any one of them.

Kenya

One of her latest Nature reserves to be designated is the Shimba Hills (47,550 acres) near the coast where the sable antelope is under special protection. This follows the discovery that only sixty sable remained, less than a quarter of the 1960 count. They were featured prominently in LIFE magazine of December 5, 1969.

Another such reserve, Marsabit, is the home of some of Africa's few remaining big tuskers with ivory weighing over 100 pounds. At the other end of the scale, Kenya is a refuge of the four-inch-long Golden Mole.

The Game Department has also mounted rescue

N

operations where Roan antelope and situtunga were under threat.

Note: "Animals," President Kenyatta told me, "are part and parcel of the prosperity of our country, and of Africa in general."

African businessmen are already running safari companies in Kenya, and soon there will be black "white" hunters.

Malawi

The Malawi National Park consists of 325 square miles on the Nyika plateau in the northern region. It contains big numbers of plains game, including zebra, eland and Roan antelope, with the occasional pride of lion or a leopard to prey on them.

In half-a-dozen game reserves and controlled areas throughout the country there are elephant, buffalo and several species of antelope and buck. The lonely Nyala antelope is a special attraction in one of them. Its head was recently featured on a local £1 stamp.

Tanzania

Serengeti (the country's only national park at the time of independence): Lion, elephant, hippo, rhino, klipspringer, dikdik, oribi, warthog, reedbuck, waterbuck, Roan antelope, wildebeest, zebra, Thomson's gazelle, Grant's gazelle, topi, buffalo, giraffe, impala, leopard, eland and many others. One unfortunate poacher there served as a grim warning to others. He fell on his own poisoned arrows while being chased by a field force, and was dead within half-an-hour.

A number of the animals in Serengeti appear to

acknowledge the African rangers as their protectors. One two separate occasions, old bull buffaloes have made their way to them when the time came to die. One lay down six feet from a rangers' hut. They tried to raise him, but he refused to leave them and died during the night. An official report on the incidents stated: "One can only surmise that, feeling death close, they feel safer near human beings than in the bush where hyena and lion would tear them to pieces."

Selous Game Reserve (15,000 square miles, and claimed to be the largest of its kind in the world): Photographic safaris are conducted there, and its forty hunting blocks are alternated for use. In the reserve are lion, elephant, leopard, rhino, buffalo, and some of the equally prized trophies such as sable antelope and the Greater Kudu. It has 900 miles of tracks for fly-in hunters. The reserve is an example of how hunting and conservation can be reconciled by supervision. But the man it remains named after epitomises the colonial figure largely blamed by Africans today ("We have killed wild animals out of hunger and necessity but not for a mere urge to create carnage and wanton destruction") for the ravaged ranks of the animals. Frederick Selous, naturalist, explorer, big-game hunter extraordinary and soldier, rode down elephant on horseback. He shot as many as 30 elephant a day with muzzle-loading rifles; and when his horse could no longer follow the herds, he would pursue them on foot, clad only in a shirt and a pair of sandals. His grave in the reserve is near where he fell during the 1914–18 war.

Rwaha National Park boasts herds of the Greater Kudu.

With the formation of a national park of 720

square miles on the higher slopes of Mount Kilimanjaro, Tanzania in a matter of a few years has added seven new parks to its roll of conservation.

The most novel and remote of her reserves is named Gombe Stream, 15 miles north of Kigoma on the eastern shore of Lake Tanganyika. Proclaimed for the protection of one of the last troops of chimpanzees in the country (their companions there are Red Colobus and putty-nose monkeys), Gombe Stream was the scene of experiments which gained wide fame. The researchers were able to show how sixty to eighty chimpanzees in Gombe (said to be the closest animal to Man) can think constructively—fashioning collected strips of grass into "fishing lines" and poking them down holes to catch ants, making sponges from chewed leaves and grass to mop up water—and so on.

Another small Tanzanian reserve (52,269 acres) is a non-predatory island in Lake Victoria where, among rain forest and in grassy glades, live chimpanzees which are being returned to the wilds from zoos in Europe. New arrivals, it seems, find it hard to adapt themselves to drinking water, after being used to sipping cups of tea daily before crowds of laughing spectators. There are also rhino and roan antelope on the island.

Notes: Perhaps the most enchanting of Tanzania's game reserves is the one which is the smallest. And it is privately owned and maintained. A mere 30 acres in size, it is situated just off the main road between Arusha and Moshi, and was started in 1961 with an antelope and a couple of crown birds. It is now a wild life wonderland in a flamboyant tropical setting. Zebra, giraffe, waterbuck and birds live in an open compound, separated from visitors only by a large, hidden ditch. Elsewhere, a Thomson's gazelle, free to wander where it likes, might be seen lying in the shade of a python's or the lions' cage while a few yards away a reedbuck relaxes beside a rhino's enclosure. At weekends, Africans make up the majority of visitors ("I suddenly realised when I started the sanctuary how few of them have the money or the time to see the animals which are Africa's greatest attraction," says the owner), and wrapt boys and girls can be seen feeding nuzzling gazelle, stroking the satin feathers of a crippled, tame eagle, or romping with a lion cub.

Lone specimens of white giraffe with no markings of any sort have been seen in Tanzania and northern Kenya.

A tribal chief is the chairman of the Board of Trustees of the Tanzania National Parks.

Uganda

The Maramgambo Forest at the southern end of Queen Elizabeth National Park is a chimpanzee sanctuary.

Note: The Chanler's reedbuck, which has a shrill whistling call, is among the novelties to be found in her national parks.

West Africa

This half of the Continent can show the visitor quite a few oddities in the animal kingdom—friendly and brash wild gorillas; the cane rat which looks like a hamster, runs like a pig and is more of a porcupine than a rodent; murderous, untamable hunting dogs from which even leopards will retreat; the yellow-backed duiker, which has straw-coloured hair along

the back to its rump and makes a nest under fallen
trees in thick forests, and the African skunk known as
the zorilla, striped in black and white along its back
and popular with country Africans as a swift killer
of poisonous snakes.

Zanzibar Island

One of the last homes on earth of the Red Colobus.

Zambia

Kafue National Park (8,650 square miles): Lion,
buffalo, and a great variety of antelope, gazelles and
buck including the rare blue-backed duiker.

Livingstone Game Park (300 acres): Lion, rhino,
giraffe and antelope can be seen against the majesty,
and double rainbows, of the Victoria Falls, along with
schools of protected hippo in the Zambezi River.
Sumbu Game Reserve (in the north, on Lake Tanganyika's Kasaba Bay): Hippo and elephant.

The Luangwa Valley Game Reserve: Black rhino,
lion, Cookson's wildebeest, leopard, Thornycroft's
giraffe, zebra, antelope, and an extensive elephant
population. Tourists, escorted by an African armed
guard, are allowed to follow the game on foot;
photographers can get thrilling close-ups of Africa's
biggest animals. Most evenings, groups of elephant
move from any denuded part of the reserve to feed an
adjacent licensed hunting area. Well aware of the
danger of lingering, they return to the reserve each
day before dawn.

Notes: Near the main camp in the Kafue National
Park stands a 100 feet tall sacred tree where long ago
warriors tested their spears before battle. Several

spear-heads can still be seen embedded in the trunk, and poker-faced African guides go through the ceremony of invoking the Spirit of the Tree and asking its permission for parties of game-viewers to pass.

Zambia offers the world's only recorded white impala, a ghostly albino flitting between the trees. It is also the locale (in the remote Bangweulu Swamps where Dr. Livingstone's heart was buried) of the black lechwe which has been on a Swiss-published international list of species in danger of extinction. The little-known puku (antelope) is also protected in Zambia. These graceful animals have a marked sense of territory. When the young are born, they are hidden in long grass and the mothers never move more than a few hundred yards away to feed. Efforts to translocate puku from riverine plains in Zambia have failed. Those which have been immobilised with tranquilliser darts and taken by African game officials to other districts have made their way back to their home territories. One female escaped by leaping an eight-foot high fence and joined other puku, homing strongly on their old habitat through miles of thicket.

Note: One of the most enjoyable, and, perhaps, safest means of getting close-ups of animals is from boats, and this can easily be done on the Zambian side of Lake Kariba. Parts of the shoreline have been declared reserves where elephant, lion, buffalo, rhino and other game—reduced in an "Animal Dunkirk" operation from shrinking islands in the floods when a dam wall was built across the Zembezi ten years ago—live out their destined spans, safe from Man-made disasters.

Index

aardvark 168, 169
aardwolf 99, 168, 169
Aberdare National Park 105
Abuko Game Reserve, 21-4
Africana magazine, quotes from, 60-1, 63-4
Albert National Park 112-3
Amboseli Game Reserve 92, 126
antelope 8, 23, 26, 27, 111, 117, 178
  Bongo 101, 152, 168, 169
  dwarf 168
  eland 111, 133, 171, 174
  gerenuk, long-necked 104
  klipspringer 172, 174
  lechwe 116-7
  marsh 168
  Nyala 118, 173, 174
  puku 178
  Roan 13, 101, 173, 174
  sable 152, 171, 173, 174
Arthur, Samuel, K. 12
ass, wild 119
Awash National Park 172

baboons 11, 13, 42-3, 105
  dog-faced 19
  Gelada 173

olive 42
  smuggling of 139
bears 84
beavers, Canadian 11
birds, migrating 13
Boy Scouts, African 32-3
Bryceson, Derek 36
buffalo 7, 8, 14, 21, 25, 70, 80, 103, 105, 115, 133, 171
  as food 51-3
  dwarf 15
  snaring 139
  trust of rangers 174-5
bush-babies 105
bushbuck 13, 23, 25, 172, 174, 177
bush cow 27
Bushmen 111
bush pig 13, 85
bustard, black-bellied 25
Bwiru Girls' School 74

Cade, C. E., "Bobby" 79
camels 11, 112
cane rat 177
cats, genet 23
  golden 99, 167
  serval 23, 42
cheetahs 14, 25, 70, 80, 86, 99, 103, 116, 167-8, 172

chimpanzees 20, 23, 27, 80,
  85, 175, 177
  diet 146
  dwarf 113
  research 176
Chobe Reserve 171
civet, spotted palm 23
  West African 23
cobras 11
College of African Wildlife
  Management 1, 3-10, 17,
  50, 71, 77, 146, 152
crocodiles 11, 13, 19, 25, 27,
  38-48, 86, 101, 103, 105
  mother care 41-2
crown birds 176
culling of game 51-5

Denis, Michaela 120-1
dibitag, see gazelle, Clarke's
dikdik 174
Director of National Parks,
  Tanzania 69-71
dogs, hunting 25, 117
  wild 70, 85
donkeys, Moroccan 32
dugong 66-8, 167
duiker 25
  black 15
  blue 88, 177
  crown 13
  Maxwell's 23
  red-flanked 13
  yellow-backed 177
Duke of Edinburgh 118, 119

eagles, fish 42, 43, 176
East African Standard 88,
  162
East African Wild Life
  Society 61, 120
educating for conservation
  71-2, 99, 137, 147, 149-
  153, 159
egret, great white 43

eland 20, 111, 133, 171, 174
elephant 8, 13, 14, 15, 20, 21,
  25, 26, 27, 70, 99, 104,
  110, 111, 133, 139, 152-7,
  171, 172, 173, 174, 175,
  177, 178
  as food 49-59
  marking 153
  poaching 16, 17
  trophies 94-7, 108
El Molo tribe 46
Emperor Haile Selassie 118

fish 56, 64-5, 155
flamingo 103, 137, 167
Food and Agricultural Organisation of U.N. 17
Ford Foundation 2, 160
fox, bat-eared 81, 104
  Simien 118, 173

game as food 49-59, 111, 116
game farms 44-8, 50-8
game hunters, big 99, 100,
  106, 111, 173, 175
game reserves, definition 164-
  6
Garamba National Park 114
gazelles 27, 85, 172, 177
  Clarke's 118
  Grant's 133, 174
  Thomson's 50, 57, 82, 103,
  133, 174, 176
gemsbok 172
giraffe 25-7, 99, 102, 105, 154,
  172, 174, 176, 177
  horned Rothschild 101
  reticulated 104
  Thornycroft's 178
  trophies 108
Goaso Game Reserve 14
Gombe Stream Reserve 175
gorillas 177
  mountain 113, 145

Grzimek, Dr. Bernhard 36
guinea pigs 11

hartebeest, Western 13, 25
hashish 109
Hemingway, Patrick 8-9, 50-1
herons, Goliath 42, 43
hippopotamus 11, 14, 19, 25,
    27, 29-37, 51-2, 99, 103,
    105, 116, 154, 174, 178
    as food 53
    pygmy 86, 117
    trophies 95, 97
hog, giant forest 168
hornbill 43, 156
hyenas 11, 25, 27, 43, 88, 133,
    175
hyrax 99

Ibex, Walia 118, 173
iguanas 11
impala 103, 172, 174, 178

jackals 22, 86, 103

Kafue National Park 177, 178
Kaggwa, Christopher 46
Katete, Francis 143, 146-9
Kaunda, President Kenneth
    51
Kenyatta, President 98, 173-4
Khama, President 172
Kidepo National Park 114
kites 42, 87
Kleburg, Jnr., Robert J. 57-8
kob 88
kongoni 103, 133
kudu 171, 175
Kujani 14

Lake Nakuru National Park
    103, 152
Lake Victoria island reserve
    176
lechwe, black 178

leopard 7, 8, 11, 13, 23, 25,
    70, 74-6, 84, 103, 106,
    116
    coats 119-21
    transporting 87-8
    trap 139
lions 1, 8, 11, 13, 70, 84, 99,
    123, 133, 139, 152
    black-maned 84, 172
    man-eating 154-5
    research 79-81
Livingstone Game Park 177
lizards, monitor 13, 23, 42-3
Luangwa Valley Game
    Reserve, 52, 178
lynx 168

Makerere University College
    136, 143
Malawi National Park 117
Malindi Marine Park 61
manatee 20, 167
Manu, Christopher 14-18
Marine national parks 60-8
Marsabit Reserve 173
Masai Amboseli Game
    Reserve 103, 127
Masai Mara Game Reserve
    104
Masai people 93, 122-42
Mbarnoti, Chief Edward 130
Meru National Park 105
Mikumi National Park 32
Mole Game Reserve 13
Mohammed, Hassan Said
    152-3
moles, golden 173
    West African 23
Monah, John Ole 76-7
mongoose, Gambian dwarf 23
    white-tailed 42, 88, 105
monkeys 23, 25, 133
    blue 116,
    green 13

green vervet 23, 86
putty-nosed 175
Red Colobus 23, 99, 119, 173, 175, 177
Moremi Reserve 172
Murchison Falls National Park 39-44, 53, 146

Nairobi National Park 103, 152, 153
national parks, definition 164-6
natural reserves, definition 165
Ndugwa, Bernard 44
Ngethe, Samuel 82-9
Ngorongoro 133
Nkrumah, Dr. Kwame 11-12
Nyerere, Julius 2, 33, 36, 71, 127, 137

Odoro, A. O. 71
Okavango Reserve 47
Olindo, Perez 150-2, 154, 158, 161
Oloitipitip, Shapashino Ole 124
oribi 13, 23, 25, 81, 174
orphanages, animal 23, 24, 78-89
ostriches 27, 80, 103, 168, 172

parrots 23
pigs, wild 19, 103
poachers 1, 8, 15, 16, 17, 20, 39, 43, 44, 86, 91-7, 100, 108-18, 139, 149, 174
porcupines 22, 23, 88
puff adders 11
pythons 11, 22, 25, 176

Quagga 169
Queen Elizabeth National Park 53, 177

reedbuck 13, 23, 85, 174, 176
Chanler's 177
research stations 44-8
rhinoceros 1, 8, 14, 80, 90-7, 99, 101, 102, 103, 105, 114, 133, 145, 149, 152, 171, 172, 174, 175, 176, 177
Riney, Thane 49-50
rock rabbit, see hyrax 99
Ruhweza, Sylvester 143-6

Saibull, Solomon ole 132-42
Samburu Game Reserve 104
sea cow see manatee
Selous Game Reserve 175
Shai Hills Game Reserve 14
sharks 65
Shimba Hills Reserve 173
situtunga 20, 168, 173
skunk, see zorilla 177
Sokoine, Edward M. 129-30
squirrels, ground 25
sun 23
Ssemwezi, Ponsiano 149-50
starlings 156
steenbok 80
storks 42, 43, 84
Sumbu Game Reserve 178

topi 174
trapping methods 33-6, 43, 108-12, 117, 139
Tsavo National Park 54-6, 104, 152, 154
Tubman, President 86
turkeys 11
turtles 167, 168
green 65-6

vipers, Gaboon 11
vultures 43, 110, 115

warthog 13, 49, 74, 86, 174
Watamu National Park 61

waterbuck 13, 14, 23, 25, 103,
   133, 171, 174
Waza National Park 27
weaver birds 156
Wild Animal Orphange,
   Kenya 78-89 *see also*
   orphanages
Wild Animals Protection Act,
   Kenya 99
wild dog 70, 85
wildebeeste 49, 86, 103, 115,
   133, 139, 174
   Cookson's 178

Wilmot, Bob 47
World Conference on
   National Parks 60

Yankari Game Reserve 24-5

Zanzibar Island 177
zebras 86, 87, 102, 114, 116,
   133, 139, 156, 168, 172,
   174, 176, 177
   as food 57
zebroids 105
zorilla 177